Social Security:
Lightly Toasted, Not Burnt

How to make your best claiming decision

Marcia MacDonald Mantell

For my incredible sister, Michele.

I so admire all you've accomplished on that crazy,
curvy road of life. Here's to memories of our Pepper Green
bedroom, that summer in Minneapolis,
and our Midwest road trip.

I wish you an amazing retirement...
it's coming around the corner fast!

Disclaimer

This book is intended solely as an educational resource. The information is based on the United States Social Security's rules and regulations publicly available in the Social Security Act and Amendments, and on Social Security's website, www.SSA.gov, as of October 2025. The U.S. Congress may amend the Social Security law at any time.

Deciding when to claim Social Security is ultimately each individual's responsibility. The information in this book may help you with your claiming decisions. Social Security has multiple components, including old age and survivor benefits, disability benefits, and Medicare. This publication only covers old age and survivor retirement benefits (OASI).

It is highly recommended that you consult with financial professionals who have expertise in Social Security matters and with your tax advisor before claiming benefits.

Only the Social Security Administration (SSA) can provide final, actual benefit amounts. The examples used throughout this book are for illustration purposes only and should be considered rough estimates. Any errors are unintentional.

Use your own Social Security statement and the tools on www.SSA.gov to estimate your own retirement benefit.

Table of Contents

Introduction 1

How This Book is Organized 5

SECTION 1
Social Security Basics: From a Bit of History
to Your Benefit Calculation 7

1. A Bit of History 9

2. Women and Social Security –
an Important Partnership 13

3. The Elephant in the Room 21

4. A Most Important Document 25

5. Getting Your Social Security
Retirement Benefit 37

6. Two Important News Flashes 47

7. How Much Do You Really Need to Know?.............. 57

SECTION 2
Four Social Security Claiming Categories 61

SECTION 2A
Information If You Are Single 63

8. Social Security for Individual Workers..................... 65

9. Making It On Your Own, Even Though
Once Married 71

10. A Life-Long Single Lady Who Wouldn't
Change a Thing 77

SECTION 2B
The Basics for Happily Married Couples 83

11. Married Couples – Coordinating
Benefits and Claiming Decisions 85

12. The "Traditional" Husband and Wife Couple 101

13. She's the Doctor, He's the Starving Artist 107

14. She's Older and Ready to Claim.
Will She Get a Spousal "Top-Up?" 113

SECTION 2C
Information for Divorced Individuals 119

15. The Basics of Claiming on Your Ex-Spouse 121

16. Divorced and Working: Should I Claim
at FRA to Help Pay the Bills? 133

17. Married for Years, then Divorced – Delighted to
Claim on Her Ex 139

SECTION 2D
Surviving Spouses Overview 145

18. Becoming a Widow or Widower 147

19. Married, Early Widowhood, Remarried,
Divorced, Surviving Ex-Spouse 163

20. Retirement Plans Cut Suddenly and
Unfairly Short 169

SECTION 3:
More Social Security Must-Know Tips 175

21. Big Changes for Those Who Also
Receive A Public Pension 177

22. More Social Security Rules to Know 183

23. Final Thoughts 197

24. Acknowledgments................................... 203

25. About the Author.................................... 205

26. Endnotes 207

Introduction

No book on Social Security would be complete without recognizing the profound contributions of two remarkable women who forever changed the face of retirement.

Frances Perkins was the key architect of the original 1935 Social Security Act and its 1939 amendments. In the 1930s, women had limited influence in government or political power. Yet, Frances, a strong advocate for women, was appointed by Franklin D. Roosevelt as his Secretary of Labor. She was the first woman to serve in the Presidential Cabinet. One of her first orders of business upon arriving in Washington was to draft the Social Security Act. By mid-1935, the proposal was complete, and Congress enacted a new law providing retirement insurance for workers. However, most workers at that time were men. She continued to work with Congress to include provisions for a social safety net for women: workers, at-home wives and mothers, and widows in their retirement years.

Before she was the "Notorious RBG," Ruth Bader Ginsburg pushed the Social Security law into modern times. An original provision in Social Security's survivor benefits only protected widows raising young children. They received survivor's benefits after losing the male breadwinner. However, when a man stayed home to raise a child after his wife's death, there were no equal benefits. Mrs. Ginsburg's argument before the Supreme Court in 1975 changed that. Her challenge to the traditional male-as-breadwinner and female-as-homemaker model shifted

1

how government benefits are distributed. As a result, women's earnings, even if often lower than men's, were finally recognized as equal dollar for dollar.

It is with gratitude and deep appreciation that all Americans benefit from the efforts of these two women. They didn't start out as heroes, but they rose to the challenges of their time to ensure future generations could depend on a level of financial support and dignity in retirement.

A time of uncertainty

Social Security celebrated its 90th anniversary in August 2025. It is by far and away the most popular federal program in the United States. However, despite its long history, there has never been such widespread concern about the solvency and future viability of the social safety net designed to provide workers with a foundation of income in retirement.

Rumors about the untimely death of Social Security run rampant today. Big, bold headlines scream, "Social Security is going bankrupt!" Much of Congress is fueling this panic by doing nothing to address Social Security's looming shortfall. Meanwhile, many folks nearing retirement are throwing in the towel and claiming benefits earlier than planned to ensure they receive some of what they've earned.

But the situation is not that dire. Rather, our most important financial social safety net is lightly toasted but not yet burnt. It's not scorched or turned to ashes. Still, much work is needed in Congress to fix Social Security and uphold its guarantees. Enough with lawmakers dragging their feet and kicking the can down the road. It's time to repair Social Security for future generations.

All this unrest raises an important question: What should you do during times of serious uncertainty and great concern? In short, that's what this book aims to help answer. It will provide you with the current facts and the right information to help you stay calm, keep working, and watch what's happening, so you have the courage and a plan to claim benefits at the best time for you.

From my travels across the country and the calls and emails I get from people in their 50s and 60s, I know many are making a lot of mistakes. There are a surprising number of misunderstandings and misperceptions about Social Security swirling out there. Near-retirees don't often fully grasp the power of the program.

Let's admit we've either been too busy to sit down and figure out how Social Security actually works, or we didn't realize we needed to. With all the uncertainty and unrest today, it's time to buckle down and understand this important law. Too many rely too heavily on what their neighbors, siblings, or cousins say about Social Security. Please don't do that.

You have no idea how many times I've had to tell people they made the wrong decision. Most Social Security claiming decisions are irrevocable. Spouses don't realize how their claim can significantly affect their spouse. Ex-spouses aren't aware they might qualify for ex-spousal benefits. Cash flow from Social Security should be maximized, but too often it isn't.

My hope is that you finish this book with a deeper understanding of Social Security than you have now. Recognize that Congress members fully understand the consequences of their inaction. They know that nearly everyone fails at retirement if Social Security's funding isn't fixed. No matter what else you might be thinking about this critical foundation of your retirement income, making sure you understand the consequences of your own claiming decisions is a top priority.

I invite you to scrape the burnt edges off our most important social insurance program and read on...

Social Security at 90: Still the bedrock of American retirement income

Most books about Social Security focus on the nitty-gritty of its rules and benefit calculations but overlook important questions like:

- How much money could I really get from Social Security?
- What are my options for claiming benefits?
- How early can I retire and start collecting Social Security?
- Can I really qualify for benefits based on my spouse's or ex-spouse's record?
- What if my benefit is higher than my spouse's?
- What happens when there is a significant age difference between spouses?
- Do I lose some of my benefits if my ex-spouse claims on my record?
- What happens if I remarry after a divorce or the death of my spouse?
- If I outlive my spouse, what happens to our benefits?

When you have a specific question about your benefits and how they will generate income in retirement, simply knowing how to calculate your Average Indexed Monthly Earnings, or AIME (pronounced like the name "Amy"), or Primary Insurance Amount, known as PIA in Social Security lingo, just doesn't cut it.

This book aims to go beyond technical details to highlight and bring to life practical information that helps people make better decisions about this important source of retirement income. Social Security becomes the foundation of financial security in old age. Very few understand how they can fully benefit from this social insurance program. Let's change that.

How This Book is Organized

There are three parts to this book:

1. **Basic information about Social Security.** You'll learn how the program works, what information you need to know before deciding when to claim your benefits, and the implications for your retirement income.

2. **Social Security's four claiming categories.** You are considered single, married, divorced, or widowed. The rules differ for each category. Jump to the section that applies to you to learn how your benefit will be calculated. You'll also find examples of people in similar situations. There's no need to read all the sections—only the one(s) that apply to you.

3. **Other important information.** Social Security benefits have many specific rules and features. In this part, you'll get an overview of other factors to consider, such as taxes and the implications of claiming early while continuing to work. There's a new section on the significant law changes enacted in early 2025 for those with public pensions. Medicare is also part of the Social Security program. You'll see where these two programs work together.

Each scenario in Part 2 is based on real questions I've received from people across the country. In most cases, the names have been changed to protect the innocent.

Keep in mind

Social Security rules are the same for men and women. Benefits depend on your personal work and wage history. The rules also apply equally to all legally married couples—whether in opposite-sex or same-sex marriages.

There is a strong connection between Social Security and personal assets. The less you receive in Social Security, the more of your own assets you'll spend to pay for retirement.

The claiming decisions you make in your early 60s will affect your financial security into your 80s, 90s, and 100s.

Most people have read the headlines or heard that Social Security might not be around for much longer. That is simply not true. Yes, the edges of the program are slightly burnt, but that doesn't mean benefit payments will stop. This book will separate fact from fiction.

Where to get more information

There is so much important information about Social Security that it could fill 1,000 pages. Instead of getting bogged down, focus on the parts of this book that apply to you, then visit my blog, Boomer Retirement Briefs, https://boomerretirement-briefs.com/, for more details. There you'll find:

- Free action plans and checklists
- Retirement planning worksheets
- Up-to-date information on Social Security law changes and analysis of various solvency options (or the lack thereof)
- Loads of information about Medicare, including a free worksheet to estimate your healthcare costs in retirement

SECTION 1
Social Security Basics:
From a Bit of History to Your
Benefit Calculation

CHAPTER 1:

A Bit of History

The Great Depression was a tumultuous period in American history, spanning from 1929 through the 1930s. The country was at one of its lowest economic points, and citizens were suffering greatly. There were few jobs available. Farms were unproductive after years of drought. If families had any savings, they vanished with the collapse of the financial and banking systems. It was all but impossible to put a roof over a family's head. To say it was a bleak time and Americans were in dire straits is an understatement. And a significant number of older people were living in abject poverty.

Years before the Great Depression, Congress was already debating whether there was a need for a social insurance program to support impoverished elderly citizens. America had transitioned from an agricultural-based society to an industrial one, and the multi-generational, family-centric structure had been replaced by an individual one. As a result, the elderly who had previously been cared for by younger family members in extended family homes found themselves old, alone, and often living in poverty.

The sudden market crash and the severity of the Great Depression sharply exposed the crisis among the elderly. Many had lost their pensions and no longer had family to depend on.

The Social Security Act becomes law of the land

In a move championed by President Franklin D. Roosevelt, Congress passed the Social Security Act of 1935. Its primary aim was to provide retired workers with a modest income base in retirement that would prevent the elderly from falling into poverty. Behind the scenes, one woman worked tirelessly to make Social Security a reality: Frances Perkins, FDR's Labor Secretary. She was the first woman to serve in a Presidential Cabinet and a strong advocate for fair wage laws, the 40-hour workweek, and protections for women and children.

From the very beginning, it was clear that Social Security was not meant to be a welfare program. Hard-working, fiercely independent American workers were not interested in hand-outs. Unless and until each worker qualified for future benefits and paid into the system, they would not receive retirement payments. Social Security insurance was designed as a "pay-to-play" system. And it remains a pay-in to get a pay-out system 90 years later.

To ensure future recipients would diligently pay into the program, Congress placed the responsibility of making contributions on employers. There was no way around the system if you worked for a covered employer. (A covered employer is one that is required to participate in Social Security. It includes most manufacturing and private employers.) Uncovered employers included farmers, individuals who hired household help, state governments, and certain unions.

Implementing a protection program for older and retired workers was critically important, and as many as possible would need to ante up and contribute.

A very different attitude today

Here's something that might seem hard to believe: In its early days, the Social Security Administration (SSA) had to run marketing campaigns to encourage workers to get a Social Security number and apply for benefits they earned. It was a major effort to educate the public and shift the culture.

Today, it's a very different story. People can't believe they have to wait until their 60s to claim their benefits, let alone understand it is generally better to wait until at least their Full Retirement Age (from ages 66 to 67) or until age 70 before claiming.

Many near-retirees are very skeptical the program will be there for them. Younger generations have all but given up hope of receiving benefits. With the unprecedented dismantling of many Social Security Administration (SSA) operations in 2025 and the dismissal of thousands of employees who serve beneficiaries, people are understandably anxious about getting their benefits.

Many want to get what's theirs as soon as possible. Too many are willing to jump into the program too early, making a critical financial mistake. Most people know the earliest age to claim Social Security retirement benefits is 62. Yet, they don't know their own Full Retirement Age or realize the dramatic reduction in benefits if they claim so early. They simply want to "grab and go." This is often the worst financial decision someone can make. The result is to lock in their smallest benefit amount from Social Security, which may become their most important income in old age.

Social Security is still critically important – 90 years later

To say this program is vital today does not do it justice. Virtually every American adult is keenly aware they will be receiving a Social Security payment. They count down the days until they can claim it. It is a crucial part of retirement income for nearly every household.

As much as people complain about Social Security's small benefit payments today, everyone wants their share. It is a massive program that becomes increasingly important each year. About 76 million Baby Boomers are either claiming Social Security retirement benefits or are about to claim them. Another 65 million Gen Xers are nipping at the Boomers' heels. Most Americans have set up their retirement years based on the fact they will receive Social Security.

The program is bigger and more important than you may realize. Take a look at the level of support it offers:[1]

- In 2025, nearly 69 million Americans will receive over $1.6 trillion in Social Security benefits.
  - 54.4 million are retired workers and their dependents
  - 6 million are survivors
  - 8.3 million disabled persons and their dependents
- 5.8 million people started receiving Social Security benefits in 2023 for the first time.
- 55% of adult Social Security beneficiaries in 2023 were women.

CHAPTER 2:

Women and Social Security –
an Important Partnership

Social Security becomes the foundation of retirement income for almost every older American. Yet the program is widely misunderstood and misinterpreted. When speaking with near-retirees, I find they are surprised to learn that Social Security benefits were not initially available to most women. And they continue to be amazed at how the program works for women.

For those who have fallen on hard times in their oldest years, Social Security does exactly what it was designed to do: keep older Americans out of poverty during their retirement years. Both men and women.

But for those who worked in low-paying jobs or didn't have the opportunity to build a sizable nest egg, retirement often feels out of reach. The majority of people facing these circumstances tend to be women. Many women, even today, are employed in lower-paying jobs like teaching, administrative support, retail, hospitality services, daycare, and elder care, among others.

A shocking fact from the Social Security Administration: "46% of all elderly unmarried females receiving Social Security benefits relied on Social Security for 90% or more of their income." This does not mean only women who were never married.

Rather, these statistics include all unmarried women later in life. Most were in fact married, some were divorced, some were living separately from a spouse, and others had always been single.

Retirement is not always the rosy dream women have hoped for. So having as much Social Security income as possible for their oldest years becomes a critical factor for many. They will need to rely on their own benefits and also depend on their husbands to make the best decisions regarding his Social Security income. Making the best claiming decision is crucial for maintaining cash flow when both spouses are alive and after the first spouse dies.

Women were dependent spouses for decades

Each generation of women makes significant contributions to those who come after. Their sacrifices open doors for their daughters and granddaughters. For the past 100 years, women have increasingly worked outside the home, building careers and earning paychecks. In 2018, 54% of women were the primary breadwinners in their households, whether married with or without children, or single parents. In 2023, 45% of mothers were breadwinners, and another 25% were co-breadwinners. Additionally, 69% of Black mothers were the primary breadwinners in their families.[2]

In 2022, 16% of wives in opposite-sex marriages were the sole or primary breadwinners, meaning their income exceeded 60% of the total household income. That's three times higher than in 1972. In 29% of opposite-sex marriages, both spouses earn roughly equal shares of income, between 40% and 60%.[3]

This marks tremendous progress for women in a relatively short time. They are becoming increasingly financially independent, which should result in higher overall Social Security benefits when they retire.

That's because future Social Security benefits are calculated based on the income earned during one's working years. A person qualifies for Social Security on their own work record. Until relatively recently, women didn't have their own work record. Instead, most women relied solely on their husbands for financial security in retirement.

It's tremendously encouraging to see how women are catching up today. By advancing in their careers and earning their own income, women become independently insured for Social Security benefits. In fact, the percentage of women who are now fully insured on their own merits has skyrocketed from 63% in 1970 to 87% in 2023. In comparison, 90% of men are fully insured in 2023.[4]

This means that more women than ever have worked long enough and earned enough income from wages or self-employment to qualify for their own retirement benefits from Social Security. This is indeed an important step forward in women's financial journeys. Yet, for many women, their monthly paycheck is significantly smaller than that of a man with the same years of work. And her monthly Social Security income is considerably lower. But it's all forward progress.

The first Social Security payment

In an interesting twist of history, the first person to receive Social Security benefits was a woman. She has become quite famous in the annals of Social Security history. Ida May Fuller was a legal secretary in Vermont. Her employer paid a total of $24.75 toward her Social Security benefits. Her first check, dated January 31, 1940, was for $22.54. How long did she receive payments? For every month that she lived in retirement – in her case, until age 100. She died in 1975 after collecting a total of $22,888.92 in Social Security benefits.[5]

15

Ida May's story highlights one of the most important features of Social Security: it delivers monthly income every month of your retirement, for as long as you live.

Shock and unhappiness

There's nothing quite like seeing the shocked looks I get when I give a presentation on Social Security. The first question I ask audiences who are age 50 and older is, "How much, on average, do Social Security recipients receive in retirement benefits each year?" The answers from audiences range from $15,000 to $50,000 per year. In other words, very few have any idea of the real amount.

When I reveal the answers, the audience audibly gasps. In 2019, the average yearly payment for men was about $19,000, while for women it was around $15,000. By December 2023, average benefits increased to roughly $25,000 for men and $20,500 for women. This equals about $1,580 per month for men and just $1,250 for women in 2019, and $2,100 for men and $1,700 for women in 2023. Women are outraged, and often one or more will shout "Why?" in disbelief.

Why women have lower Social Security payments

Why, indeed. When you think about your own life's journey, you might remember some years when you stayed home to raise your children or to care for an aging parent or relative. You may have taken on part-time or lower-paying jobs to meet the needs of your household. Perhaps it took 20 years to climb the career ladder, or you chose to pursue a Ph.D. that took five or six years away from your earnings. Whatever your personal path, most women find that it was not a straight line. With all the demanding roles women must play, they often don't have a continuous career where income starts high and increases every year. It was more of a winding path. Some might even say it was more curvaceous.

It turns out, however, that each person's wages, earnings history, and specific career path significantly influence their Social Security payments decades later. You might be surprised to learn that Social Security is designed to be fair, even though it often doesn't seem fair when you compare benefits. One reason many women feel they are treated unfairly is that they weren't aware of Social Security's rules and how benefits are calculated based on their earnings. Many men are also surprised at how much less their wives will bring to the retirement income party. And their own benefits aren't nearly as large as they expected after 40 or more years of hard work.

We need to ask why anyone would focus on Social Security benefits in their 20s, 30s, or 40s. After all, in those early years, we're busy building a life, a career, and often a family. Thinking about how our choices impact retirement isn't on the table.

Understand key aspects of the program

Let's put Social Security into perspective and highlight some key aspects of the program. It is, and always has been, a social insurance program. It was important to the architects of this program that it would not be a welfare program. Social Security would be an earned benefit that each American worker could qualify for based on their own personal work and earnings history.

The 1939 Social Security Amendments expanded eligibility for payments. Initially, retirement income benefits were only paid to the worker. However, from the 1930s through the 1970s, most American women married, had children, and stayed home to raise those children and run the household. They had no earnings record and did not contribute directly to Social Security. Yet Congress acknowledged in the law that women played a crucial role in the economic success of a household.

Managing a home and raising children had real value, even though women didn't earn paid wages for this work. At retirement, a woman's household contributions were nonetheless credited based on her husband's earnings record. A married woman was entitled to her own Social Security check and could receive up to half of her spouse's full retirement benefit. (We might argue that at-home moms should get twice their husbands' benefits, but the formula doesn't work that way!)

The benefit formula for retirement is based on each worker's highest 35 years of average earnings. Your actual Social Security payment amount is, therefore, directly linked to your work history over several decades. Many women, however, have had "popcorn" work histories—they've popped in and out of the workforce while juggling obligations at home. That's why, on average, women tend to receive smaller monthly payments. They simply haven't worked for paid wages long enough or earned as much income. Yet.

You can still influence your Social Security payment

If you are still quite a few years away from retiring, you might be able to increase your benefit amount. This happens when you continue working and earning more each year. If you are close to retirement, your benefit amount is basically set.

You'll want to review your most recent benefit estimate, which you can find on your Social Security statement. To access your statement and protect your Social Security number from cyber trolls, other bad apples, and hackers, it's very important to set up an account at Social Security's website. Look for the "my Social Security" icon on the homepage or use the direct URL: www.ssa.gov/myaccount. It only takes a few minutes to create your account.

If you created your account years ago and haven't visited it recently, please go online. The method to access your account has changed, and starting in 2025, you can no longer use a username and password. You need to set up a new access point with LOGIN.GOV or ID.ME.

Once you have your statement, review your work history. How many years of earnings do you have? What is your estimated benefit amount at retirement? How much less would you get if you claim before your Full Retirement Age? How much more if you wait until 70?

You can then decide how much longer you want to work based on what you see on your statement. It may be beneficial to keep working as your benefits could increase significantly. You might also determine that your work history is sufficient, and now you know how much to plan for in retirement. Additionally, you may qualify for higher benefits based on your spouse's record. Your statement is an excellent tool to help you make these decisions.

The moment of truth

Oftentimes, attending a Social Security presentation or webinar is the first time nearly retired folks face the reality of what it means to create retirement income. It's surprising when they realize they aren't going to get a heck of a lot of income from Social Security. Call it a moment of truth.

Whether Social Security will be a significant amount of your retirement paycheck or not, it is an excellent program for older Americans. It serves as a social safety net that is vital for most retirees and their families. For the past 90 years and counting, Social Security has been the bedrock of Americans' retirement security.

It is not, and never was, intended to be a replacement for wages earned through work or self-employment. It was, however, designed to keep some of our most vulnerable citizens out of poverty, and provide each worker and their spouse with a modest income throughout retirement. Plan accordingly.

CHAPTER 3:

The Elephant in the Room

Before diving into more details about planning for your Social Security retirement benefits, let's address the elephant in
the room. Many people are understandably worried about the
Social Security program and wonder—and doubt—if it will
still be around for them. It's smart to question the program's
viability, but it's even more important to get the facts. The media hype and hoopla are an ongoing problem. The sensational
headlines can stop anyone in their tracks. But rarely do they
provide enough facts to help us understand the real situation.
Let's get to the bottom of it all.[6]

- The Social Security Administration forecasts the program
  will be here for the long haul. Their projections look
  forward 50 and 75 years at a time.

- Current funding by workers via Federal Insurance Contributions Act (FICA) supports payments to the current
  retirees.

- The Social Security trust fund was tapped for the first
  time in the 1980s. Back in 1982, the trust fund "went
  bankrupt." Only then did Congress act to modernize
  Social Security and ensure it would pay full benefits for
  the next 50 years.

- Now, in the 2020s, Social Security can only pay 100%
  of earned benefits by tapping the savings account (tech-

nically called the "reserve account") within the trust fund. Since 2021, retirees receive full benefits funded by incoming payroll contributions plus reserve assets.

- In the 2025 Trustees Report, the actuaries project the reserve account will run out by 2033. However, additional changes from Congress and shifts in employment are likely to cause full depletion earlier than 2033.

- Beneficiaries will keep receiving payments after 2033, but they will be decreased if Congress does nothing to shore up the system.

- The current projection shows payments will be cut by roughly 23% for everyone receiving old-age retirement or survivor benefits starting in 2033.

- If you won't be old enough to claim by 2033, assume the benefit estimates shown on your current Social Security statements could be reduced.

The big message here is that Social Security will continue for more years than you will be alive. As long as you otherwise qualify for retirement benefits, you will receive them. They will still be based on your personal work history. However, they could be reduced if Congress fails to take strategic and specific action. And they need to act soon.

Time to get in the game

What are the most important steps all of us Baby Boomers, Gen Xers, and Millennials can do to stay on top of Social Security's solvency? There are many ways to get involved and stay informed, including these three recommendations.

1. **Get to know your representatives and senators.** Call them often. Email them. Join the AARP lobby group to keep pressure on Congress to do the right things to shore up Social Security. Each of our voices is import-

ant. Collectively pressing our legislators can move the needle. As we've seen lately, we might also need to protest to defend Social Security. Some will march on Washington. Many more will stand outside their local field office and rally to protect our earned benefits. "Keep your hands off our Social Security!" is a common message on protestors' signs. It really is time to lace up your sneakers and join a rally.

2. **Understand the Social Security Act is a law.** It can only be changed by an act of Congress. (I guess that's better than needing an act of God, but sometimes it seems to be on the same order of magnitude.) The last major overhaul of Social Security took place during the Reagan administration in 1983. That's the last time the funding and solvency of Social Security's trust fund were threatened. The changes Congress made in 1983 provided security until 2034, supporting the program for 50 years. Surely, our Congress can propose solutions for Social Security's current challenges to keep it healthy for the next 50 years. In fact, there are over a dozen excellent ideas already on the table and available to fix Social Security. There is simply a serious lack of political will to implement these reasonable solutions.

3. **Get the facts, ma'am.** Don't let the headlines cause you alarm. Go to primary sources to get your facts. See what individual representatives and senators are proposing. Check what Social Security is recommending. Get your facts from the horse's mouth. The best page on Social Security's website for this information is www.ssa.gov/OACT/solvency. There you'll find the latest proposals about Social Security's solvency circulating through the legislative process. Stay informed about what your representative is supporting (or not), and make sure you let them hear from you. On a topic

as important as your income in retirement, every voice and vote counts.

Since 2018, I've been writing about this very issue of Social Security solvency in mainstream media and on my blog, Boomer Retirement Briefs. You can read them (and many other posts) at https://boomerretirementbriefs.com.

CHAPTER 4:

A Most Important Document

It's easy to find out if you are eligible for Social Security retirement benefits and how much you might receive by reviewing your most recent statement. To access your statement, you'll need to register on Social Security's website if you haven't already. You'll need to create your *"my Social Security"* online account—or update your access with the latest technology. In fact, I believe it is so important that you take this step, I'm going to suggest you put this book down for five minutes, grab your cell phone or log in to your computer, and visit www. ssa.gov/myaccount to open your account. It is fast, easy, and essential.

Starting in 2025, you'll need to use either LOGIN.GOV or ID.ME to verify your identity more securely. The old username and password will no longer be available.

What's in a statement?

Take a close look at your statement. It's a trip down memory lane. When you see 1979 as the first year you worked and earned that whopping $125, you'll hardly believe it was that long ago that you worked at McDonald's or Burger King, Woolworths or JCPenney. You will want to make sure all your personal information on your statement is correct, including:

Your name. It may seem obvious, but with marriages, divorces, remarriages, voluntary name changes, etc., it is easy to forget to update your Social Security records to reflect your current legal name.

Your date of birth. Check to make sure there are no typos in your full date of birth. You need to see the right year, with the right month and day, and that nothing is off by one digit.

Your work history. The IRS and Social Security share work and payroll/wage information. Today, this process is automated and seamless, but back in the 1970s, 1980s, and 1990s, "uploading" your data was manual data entry.

Oh no – there's a mistake on my record!

What if you find a mistake on your Social Security statement? Well, it's up to you to get it corrected.

Updating your name or date of birth requires submitting original proof documents like your birth certificate, passport, marriage license, or divorce decree, and then applying for a new Social Security card.

Where it becomes more difficult is correcting wage history. If you catch the error within the first year or two, you can call the SSA and ask for a correction. Technically, you have exactly three years, three months, and 15 days to fix wage data. And no, I didn't make up that rule.

If you find errors from years or decades ago, Social Security is not obligated to update that information — your window has closed. However, if you can provide original W-2s or your original tax returns, you can submit them and request corrections. There's no guarantee of success, but it's worth trying.

Before you deep-dive into those dusty boxes in the basement or cobweb-covered piles in the attic, make sure you need to make such a grand effort. If the missing year was likely one with low earnings and wouldn't be included in your highest 35 years of earnings anyway, don't bother. But if it was a high-earning year that could replace a $0 year, and you have the original documents, and submitting them would make you feel better, go ahead and put in the effort.

Remember, you can no longer just walk into the SSA field offices. You'll need to make an appointment in advance. In 2025, expect the wait to be 30 to 40 days to see an agent.

A few things to note about your Social Security earnings record:

Some wages seem to be missing. If you are a high earner, you'll notice that not all of your wages are listed in the "Earnings Taxed for Social Security" column. They've been capped at the annual taxable wage base (TWB), which is the amount of your income subject to Social Security taxes. Not all income is subject to Social Security FICA.

Some years may show zeroes. Over a 45-year history, you might notice specific years when you had no earned income. Whether staying home to raise your children or spending years in graduate school, it's common for many to have zeroes in their work record. This is especially true for women. If you worked for an "uncovered employer," you were not paying into the Social Security system – more zeroes.

Unemployment is not income. Many people have been laid off at some point in their careers and received unemployment benefits. "Unemployment" is technically a form of insurance, and therefore not considered wages. Social Security payroll taxes are only collected on wage income.

Disability insurance does not count as income. For moms, you might see a significant drop in your income during the years your babies were born. That's because "maternity leave" falls under the disability insurance rules. Again, insurance isn't regarded as income.

The big message here is: don't panic if you notice some gaps and zeroes. Your first reaction might be that your Social Security statement is incorrect. It probably isn't. It's just that you've done many different things over the past 40, 45, or 50 years. Not all of those things were paid jobs.

A note about the taxable wage base (TWB)

Your statement reports your earned income each year, including any zeros, up to the taxable wage base. The taxable wage base is a specific income amount on which you paid FICA taxes. Your income is capped for Social Security FICA tax purposes, and this cap changes every year.

For example, in 2019, the taxable wage base was $132,900. In 2025, it is $176,100. If you earn less than the TWB, all your earnings will be reported in the column labeled "Earnings Taxed for Social Security." If you earn more, your Social Security wages will stop at the TWB. Your Social Security taxes are paid based on your income. Once you exceed the taxable wage base, no additional Social Security taxes are due for that year.

Take a look at your wage history. If you know you earned more than what's shown on your statement, it means your FICA taxes were stopped at the TWB for that year.

You can see your total earnings for any given year in the Medicare column. After 1965, Medicare was included in FICA payroll taxes. There is no taxable wage base for Medicare Part A contributions. Therefore, your entire income is reported separately in the column labeled "Earnings Taxed for Medicare (since 1966)."

For an excellent book on Medicare, you might enjoy reading my "Creating Your Medicare Recipe: Enrolling on Time and Without Penalties," available on Amazon and Barnes & Noble.

Social Security's magic number: 35

When reviewing your statement, the first thing you should check is whether you already have 35 years of earnings. That's the magic number for Social Security benefits. Social Security selects the highest 35 years of your earnings from your work history to calculate your retirement benefit.

Depending on your current age and how many years you've worked, your statement will reflect different data. Your specific information will be used to determine your estimated benefits. Where do you stand today?

If you have 35 years or more of work history earnings: You'll see dollars in at least 35 years since your earnings were first recorded. If you've stopped working, Social Security has your final data to calculate your benefits. If you continue working, your new wages will be added to your work history each year.

If you have between 10 and 34 years of work history: You either have more years of work ahead or you have finished your career. Assuming you've finished working, Social Security will use your reported wages to calculate your retirement benefit. The calculation will include zeros among your highest 35 years of history. For example, if you stayed home for 10 years raising your children and worked for 25 years, you have 35 years to consider. The difference is that 10 of those years will consist of zeros.

If you have between one and 10 years of work history: You have not yet qualified for your own benefits. You might be able to receive benefits as a spouse, ex-spouse, or surviving spouse. However, there will not be an estimate of benefits shown on your statement.

If you have no years of work history. There are several situations where you might find your entire statement filled with zeroes, including but not limited to the following:

- You worked for a state or local government. Many are "uncovered" employers who do not pay into the Social Security system. You'll receive a state pension instead. And if you qualify for spousal or ex-spousal benefits, you'll now be able to receive up to 50% of your spouse's or ex-spouse's calculated benefit. (See more about the WEP and GPO repeal in Section 3.)

- You worked for a union that chose not to participate in Social Security. In these cases, you'll receive a pension from the union instead of Social Security during retirement.

- You worked for the railroad. There is a separate retirement program that the railroad established around the same time Social Security began. Railroad workers receive a pension similar to, but separate from, Social Security.

- You were married and did not need to work outside the home. Your statement will display a series of zeros, but you might still qualify for benefits as a spouse, ex-spouse, or surviving spouse.

Key points regarding your statement

Keep in mind when reviewing your statement that your situation is unique. Your career might have many twists and turns, or you could have spent 47 years with the same employer. Use your statement to understand your own situation.

Social Security will base your benefits on 35 years of earnings. You might have exceptions that lead to lower benefits or no benefits at all. We will highlight some of these situations more closely in later chapters.

Use your statement to make "work versus retirement" decisions. If you have 10 zeros and you're 55, should you work another 10 years to replace those zeros with earnings? How much will it affect your monthly income? You need to run the numbers using the calculators on https://www.ssa.gov/benefits/calculators/ to understand the real impact on your benefit. Or work with a financial advisor experienced in Social Security. Remember, each year of wages accounts for only 1/35 of your benefit calculation, so the actual difference may not be as large as you expect.

A married woman's dilemma and disappointment

Married or previously married women often feel disappointed when they find out they don't qualify for Social Security benefits based on their own work records. They wonder whether they should try to find a job and work for the next six or seven years, now that they are 58.

My response is always a question: "Do you want to work outside the home?" Almost every time, they answer, "No." They face the dilemma of feeling disappointed and discouraged because they won't receive any Social Security benefits on their own, yet they don't want to start working at this late stage. It stings less when they learn that if they are or were married, they will indeed get their own Social Security checks. The amount will be based on the work record of their spouse or qualifying ex-spouse.

A related question has to do with the zeros. Those with 30 years of work and wages who want to retire now with their spouses or partners ask if they should just stay in their jobs and keep working until they reach 35 years of earnings.

My answer here is always the same: Run the numbers! Use the calculators at https://www.ssa.gov to see how much difference it will make to your monthly income if you work for another four or five years. Younger spouses and partners often want to join their retiring partner—including spouses in a same-sex marriage—and start their retirement lives together.

So, why continue working if you can afford to leave the job? The challenge becomes how to set up a bridge strategy until Full Retirement Age (FRA), which is the optimal time to claim retirement benefits.

Meet Michele: using her Social Security statement helped with career decisions

So many women's journeys are filled with twists and turns. In Michele's case, she was married, then separated, and eventually divorced. She has two daughters whom she treasures. They are grown, college-educated, and well on their way to building their own careers. But helping them reach adulthood was riddled with challenges and interesting opportunities. In the early years, her husband worked full-time on the "B" shift from 3:00 to 11:00 p.m., while she worked part-time from 8:00 a.m. to 2:00 p.m. That way the girls could have great care with both Mom and Dad.

Then, the family had an opportunity to move to Asia for 2 ½ years for his job. It was an exciting adventure. Michele was happy to give up her job for such an incredible opportunity for her family. After a year abroad, she did find a job in Tokyo, but it didn't include any contributions toward Social Security. Nor would she be earning a pension from this position.

Going solo

Then, after 15 years of marriage, the relationship had ended, and Michele and her husband separated. Michele became a single mother. She successfully guided her daughters through their high school and college years while working in a middle management position at a struggling company. Wages didn't go up for many of those years, and promotions were put off year after year. Moving wasn't an option at that time, and the local job market offered few alternatives.

Throughout her 40s, she managed to keep everything together with grace and good humor. She stuck to a budget, launched her girls, and found time to volunteer at her church and in networking groups. She even took a part-time job at a retail cooking store after her younger daughter went to college. It wasn't for the money, though the extra income was nice. It was a way to explore future opportunities, meet new people, and get good discounts on her favorite cooking supplies.

A surprise 50th birthday gift

On her 50th birthday, Michele received a surprise "early retirement package" offer from her long-time employer. In fact, the offer arrived in her email at the same time her 25th anniversary gift from the company landed on her desk. Yes, there certainly were twists and turns on her journey.

She jumped at the chance to find a new direction in her career. She wouldn't be retiring early, but she was happy to accept the early-out package. Now, she faced some critical decisions. What types of jobs would she want to pursue? Would this new position need to offer a higher salary? Or could she start to scale back or work part-time? Could she pursue something she was more passionate about? Or were the economic realities her top priority?

Using her Social Security statement as a decision-making tool

One tool Michele used during the evaluation was her Social Security statement. What she saw in terms of her estimated benefits did not make her do the happy dance. At age 50, Michele had only 32 years of earnings under her belt. So close to the magic number... and yet so far. She saw that many of those years were from high school and college – part-time, minimum-wage jobs. Then, there were the early career years, followed by part-time work while she was raising her girls. There were three years of zeroes while living in Asia, but her last 10 years looked pretty good.

Furthermore, while she meets the requirements as an ex-spouse and may be able to claim a higher benefit based on her ex's record, she was, in fact, the higher earner. Therefore, Michele's highest Social Security benefit will come from her own work record. She's not aiming to be a millionaire but wants to ensure she has a reasonably comfortable retirement. By analyzing her statement, she could clearly see that the next 10 to 15 years would be critical earning years for her. A much larger Social Security check was possible. She had enough time.

So, Michele focused on finding a job where she could make as much money as possible. This wasn't the time to scale back her career or accept a lower-paying position. Her passion projects and hobbies that could generate income would have to wait. That paycheck during her 50s was going to be essential.

She set her sights on leveraging all her years of experience, learned the new skills needed to find a job in the high-tech era, and landed a great position that even involved some travel. It was a well-deserved opportunity. She's young at heart, eager to take on new challenges, and looking forward to a much larger Social Security retirement benefit at her Full Retirement Age (FRA) than might have been the case if she hadn't carefully reviewed her statement when she turned 50.

When was the last time you looked at your statement?

Michele's story isn't meant to suggest you should get a new job. It's meant to show that every woman has her own unique journey that might look very different from most men's career paths. While we can appreciate someone else's story, we each create our own. Social Security will only look at your situation when calculating your benefits. They are very clear about how they approach the math using your numbers. It's up to you to embrace your journey.

By using your own statement to your advantage, you can make better decisions. You might work longer, or you might retire before finishing this book. Perhaps you were thinking about claiming your benefit at age 62, but looking at your statement shows you how much more you'll receive by waiting until your FRA. If you are married or divorced, you can use your statement as a benchmark to see if you are eligible for a larger monthly benefit as a spouse or ex-spouse. This comparison applies to each individual. A lower-earning husband may qualify for higher benefits based on the higher-earning wife's record. This is the case with Michele's ex-husband. He will get a spousal top-up based on her record, adding to his own lower benefit. (More on spousal benefits coming up in Section 2.)

For a few sheets of paper, your statement is the most valuable tool you have in your retirement income toolbox. Sign in to www.ssa.gov/myaccount and open your statement. Read it thoroughly and use it to make good decisions for yourself and your future.

Remember, starting in 2025, there will be a new required method to access your online information. You'll need to update your old login method and use either LOGIN.GOV or ID.ME.

CHAPTER 5:

Getting Your Social Security Retirement Benefit

As a social insurance program, we're required to contribute to the system during our working years to receive benefits in our later, retirement years. You need to pay in today to get benefits tomorrow, and you must meet certain requirements to qualify. These requirements aren't difficult, but they are non-negotiable. There are no stress tests or anything overly complicated.

Here is the list of basic requirements individual workers must satisfy to become fully insured and qualify for and receive Social Security retirement benefits:

- You work for a covered employer.
- FICA taxes are contributed on your behalf with each paycheck.
- You've earned 40 credits.
- You've reached age 62.
- You are a U.S. citizen or qualifying Green Card holder.
- If you are a spouse or ex-spouse, you might be eligible for benefits based on your spouse's or ex's record.

Working for a "covered" employer

Depending on the jobs you've held, you worked for either a "covered" employer or an "uncovered" employer. "Covered" means that the employer paid into FICA – the Federal Insurance Contributions Act. "Uncovered" means your employer did not pay into FICA.

You have no control over how an employer decides to support workers' retirement plans. For instance, 15 states currently manage their own teacher pension plans through teachers' unions. Instead of paying FICA taxes and contributing to Social Security, teachers and their unions make payments directly to their pension plans. They are employed by an "uncovered" employer. There are other cases as well—if you work for certain unions, your state or local government, or in any role where an employer provides a public pension.

Some workers have or had a "hybrid" career, where they worked for both covered and uncovered employers. In that case, they might receive both a state or public pension and their earned Social Security benefit without reductions to offset the public pension. This change took effect in 2025 under the Social Security Fairness Act. More details follow in Section 3.

An important note: Some companies and organizations are both covered employers that pay into Social Security and sponsors of a private pension plan. If your employer supports both types of retirement plans and you are eligible for both, you will receive a pension plus your Social Security calculated benefits. This combination is particularly advantageous for those with that specific arrangement.

What exactly is FICA?

FICA, or the Federal Insurance Contributions Act, is the law that funds Social Security and Medicare. To pay future Social Security retirement benefits, the Federal Government needed a way to collect contributions. Instead of relying on taxpayers to voluntarily pay, the Federal Government required employers to handle the payments: they must withhold a fixed percentage of each worker's paycheck and send it to Social Security with each pay cycle. Additionally, employers are required to contribute a payment from their operating budget for each employee. Usually, the employee's contribution is matched by the employer, but this is not always the case.

Today, employees have 6.2% of their salary withheld and contributed to Social Security. Their covered employer matches that same percentage, adding another 6.2% to the system. During the Great Recession of 2008–2009, one way the Federal Government tried to boost workers' income was by lowering FICA tax payments for employees. This meant that, for two years, workers contributed only 4.2%, while the employer still paid the full 6.2%.

Raising the FICA rate is a common consideration in Congress as a way to address Social Security's funding issues. It has been proposed that both workers and employers increase their contributions. This proposal is often seen as controversial. On one side, Social Security needs more revenue. On the other side, raising the rate is viewed as an additional burden on younger workers and employers.

Those of us in the industry have known for over 30 years that solvency was a problem. If only Congress had acted 10, 15, or 20 years ago to slightly raise the FICA rate, we wouldn't be in this dilemma. But they didn't act. Now, we all face an uphill, much more difficult and urgent challenge to find a solution.

You need to earn 40 credits to qualify for benefits

Another requirement for qualifying for your own Social Security benefits is that you must earn 40 credits. A credit is worth a specific dollar amount. You earn one credit for each quarter in which you've earned a minimum income and paid FICA taxes on that income. Self-employment earnings count toward earning credits, as does paid military service.

In 2019, the minimum salary needed to earn one credit was $1,360. By 2025, this amount was $1,810. Each year, the wages required to earn a credit increase due to wage inflation. Whether you work full-time, part-time, or have a seasonal job, as long as you earn at least the specified amount, you will receive one credit.

You can earn up to four credits per year. To do so, you needed to earn at least $5,440 in 2019 and $7,240 in 2025. You don't have to work in all 12 months or for the whole year to earn credits. Credits don't have to be earned consecutively. Social Security considers the wages your employer reports for the entire year. If those wages are higher than $7,240, you've earned all four credits, regardless of which month or months you worked. For example, if you earned $2,000 in January and $2,000 in March, you'll earn two credits in 2025.

Age 62 opens the Social Security gate

I have yet to meet anyone in America who doesn't know the earliest age to start Social Security. "It's 62!" they shout out with glee. Yes, that is correct. Once individuals reach age 62, Social Security opens access to retirement benefits. Many people anxiously await their 62nd birthday so they can check out of their jobs and jump into the lap of luxury called retirement.

- In 2020, approximately 55% of men and 59% of women claimed their benefits before reaching their Full Retirement Age (28% of men and 31% of women claimed benefits at the earliest age of 62).

- In 2024, 60% of men claimed benefits before FRA, and 62% of women did the same (26% of men and 28% of women claimed at 62).

The problem with claiming early is that it locks in a significant and permanent decrease to monthly income. For the entire length of one's retirement.

The question we should be asking isn't, "How quickly can I get my hot little hands on my Social Security check?" but rather, "Is there a catch to taking my Social Security at 62?" That is the critical question, and most people don't know to ask it.

When it looks too good to be true...

It's important to understand and remember that Social Security is designed to provide only a modest income in retirement. It serves as a safety net, not an income replacement. Your personal retirement income payment from Social Security is a calculated benefit called the Primary Insurance Amount or PIA.

The calculated value is the amount you receive only if you claim at your Full Retirement Age (FRA). That's the age Social Security considers your "official retirement age"—whether you're retired from work or not. Think of this age as the anchor for your benefit calculation. Your FRA depends on your birth year and ranges from 66 to 67. Some might have an FRA of 66 and 8 months, for example. Those additional months count.

Ideally, most workers should aim to claim their benefits at FRA. That's when they get their optimal amount of income. But what if they can't wait until 66 or 67? Perhaps they lose their job or need to leave work to care for a spouse or aging parents. That's why Social Security allows access once you've reached 62. The gate truly opens. However, you won't get the amount of money you expected. In fact, you will face a significant reduction in your monthly payments. And it's a permanent reduction.

- If your FRA is 66, but you claim at 62, you'll get a permanent 25% reduction in monthly income from Social Security.

- If your FRA is 67, and you claim at 62, your penalty is a whopping 30% decrease in monthly income. Forever.

When you claim your own benefit early, the reduction formula depends on how many months before FRA you claim. There is one reduction factor during the first 36 months before FRA and a different one for months 37 to 60 as follows:

- 5/9 of 1% for each month during the first 36 months (20% reduction); plus

- 5/12 of 1% for each month that falls in the next 24 months (10% further reduction).

It turns out claiming Social Security at age 62 is a major financial decision. Sadly, I see many people so eager to quit their jobs and start collecting that they never ask, "Is there a catch?"

When to retire and when to claim are two distinct decisions

It is pretty common to think that when you retire you should immediately begin Social Security payments. This is not the case. There are two distinct decisions each person will make:

- When to quit their job.

- When to begin Social Security payments.

Keeping these two decisions separate helps clarify the importance of Social Security as a key income source for retirement. If you want to retire at 60 or 62 – and many are completely burnt out from stressful jobs – that is one decision. How you will pay your bills requires a plan and some financial strategy. You might:

- Draw from your retirement savings accounts.

- Have planned for early retirement and have a "retiring early" account set aside.

- Buy a fixed-income annuity that will provide income for six or seven years.

- Be married, and your spouse's income can support your household's finances and lifestyle.

- Have paid off your mortgage and can use that newfound money to replace your wages.

- Take on part-time work or a new job that is less physically demanding or stressful.

Unfortunately, what happens all too often is that workers leave their jobs and paychecks on a Friday and apply for Social Security benefits on Monday. If they are younger than their FRA, they permanently lock in lower (often much lower) monthly benefit amounts from Social Security. This is not the best move for most people. They simply didn't realize there are two separate decisions to consider.

There's no "bumping up" with Social Security

Remember the telephone game we played as kids? The first person in a line would whisper a sentence to the next person. Then person two would whisper the sentence to person three, and so on to the end of the line. When you asked the last person what they were told, it rarely resembled the original sentence. Person one might have said, "We're getting out of school at 2:00 today," but the last person might have heard, "They're closing school for two months."

That's what happens with the Social Security rules. One person thinks they understand the program, then tells the next, who thinks they've got it. They tell the next... and before you know it, Social Security is supposed to pay each of us $2 million.

So many people have heard that they can claim reduced benefits when the gates open at 62, then their benefit amount will be bumped up to their full payment amount once they reach FRA. That is incorrect. There is no bumping up payments once you've claimed Social Security early.

Once you claim, you're locked in

The Social Security Administration is very clear in its documentation, examples, and illustrations of how the system works. Once you're in, you're in. Whatever amount you're receiving is your permanent base payment. You will get small increases each year for cost-of-living adjustments, but those are modest adjustments to help offset inflation. Think 1% to 3%, in that range. Although during the COVID-19 pandemic, inflation reached highs we haven't seen in 40 years. That resulted in much higher COLAs in 2021 and 2022, at 5.9% and 8.7% respectively.

There are two exceptions to the permanence of your claim if you're willing to give up payments. You can stop your claim within the first 12 months and repay all benefits. This is a "do-over." Alternatively, at Full Retirement Age (FRA), you can suspend your benefits and restart them at age 70. This allows your reduced benefits to increase with delayed retirement credits.

One additional situation may apply to some married workers who have a smaller benefit and a larger spousal benefit. In these cases, the lower earner might choose to claim their own reduced benefit as early as age 62, then receive a spousal top-up later after the higher earner claims their benefit. (See the chapter on claiming as married coming up later in Section 2.)

Think carefully and strategically about whether claiming Social Security at 62 is the best path for you to take. You are, in fact, making a monumental financial decision in your early 60s that will affect your income well into your 80s and 90s. And for those who reach 100, you'll want a larger check from Social Security in your later years.

Social Security retirement benefits for citizens and Green Card holders

The final general rule for securing your retirement benefits is that you must be an American citizen. This is often obvious, but with such interesting diversity and immigration, this question comes up more often. I mostly hear it from naturalized citizens who have brought their foreign-born parents to live with them, or from foreign-born workers married to American-born spouses, or from permanent non-residents.

To qualify for Social Security, you personally – and each individual collecting – must be an American citizen or a permanent legal resident. For internationals who have become permanent residents of the U.S. and hold a Green Card, if you meet the other eligibility rules, you are generally entitled to Social Security benefits. You can receive them either as an individual worker who earned at least 40 credits or as a spouse of an eligible worker.

To ensure you understand the rules specific to your situation, anyone holding a Green Card or residing in the U.S. as a permanent resident should consult Social Security or an immigration lawyer. If you have earned Social Security benefits, make sure you and your spouse are receiving them. In most cases, if you are a permanent resident of the U.S., the same Social Security benefit rules that apply to citizens also apply to you. (However, there are many changes to eligibility for Medicare and Medicaid in HR 1, the budget bill that passed in 2025. It is critical that you check your individual status regarding how the laws may be different for immigrants.)

You should also work closely with an immigration lawyer regarding any benefits earned in the country where you were born. The U.S. and about 30 other countries coordinate retirement benefits for workers through agreements called "Totalization." If there is an agreement between your birth country and the U.S., your benefits will be recalculated according to the terms of that agreement.

In 2025, many immigrants are concerned about changes to their legal status. The best step if you are not U.S.-born is to consult an immigration attorney. You want to ensure you know the current status of your Social Security benefits, including access to Medicare Part A and Part B.

CHAPTER 6:

Two Important News Flashes

Math Is Involved and It's Not Really Your Money

As a social insurance program, Social Security requires the same level of expertise as other types of insurance: great math minds and actuaries. This is a good thing. Most of us have no idea what actuaries do or how they arrive at their projections. There are several interesting challenges a Social Security actuary must juggle when assessing the program's long-term viability and ensuring you receive your monthly payment, including:

- How can millions of beneficiaries count on a guaranteed income?

- What happens when a person's situation changes from single to married or married to widowed, for example?

- When exactly should someone be considered retired?

- What adjustments should be considered for wage inflation?

- How much of a reduction should be applied to those who want to claim early?

In other words, actuaries are concerned with how to make an insurance program sustainable and fair for decades into the future.

Finding your Full Retirement Age

The actuaries at Social Security estimate the total benefit each recipient could get, assuming they live a long time in retirement. Think of Social Security as insurance against living a long time. If you are among those who will live into your 80s, 90s, and beyond, you will face longevity. Having insurance payments arrive every month becomes incredibly important.

The actuaries begin their calculations at the anchor ages—Full Retirement Age (FRA). If you choose to claim your benefit early, you can. However, since your payments will need to last over a longer period of time, your monthly benefit amount will be reduced.

Until 1983, 65 was the magic age for everyone. It was everyone's FRA. Today, each person's FRA depends on their birth year. Here is a list for those born in 1943 and later:

Year You Were Born	Full Retirement Age (FRA)
1943-1954	66
1955	66 and 2 months
1956	66 and 4 months
1957	66 and 6 months
1958	66 and 8 months
1959	66 and 10 months
1960 and later	67

Find the year you were born to see when Social Security considers you to be retired. If you were born in 1958, your FRA is the month and year when you turn exactly 66 years and 8 months old. For example, if your birthday is June 3, 1958, you reach your FRA in February 2025. You do not reach FRA in June 2024, when you turn 66. There is no rounding off of FRA ages. In this example, you do not qualify for full, unreduced retirement benefits until you are 8 months past your 66th birthday.

What if your birthday is on the first day of the month? In that case, your FRA is anchored on the previous month. And if your birthday is January 1st of any year, your FRA was reached in December of the previous year. Yes, really.

Good News. Bad News.

When you decide to claim your benefit can have a significant impact on your financial stability throughout retirement.

Let's start with the bad news. If you claim your benefit before reaching your FRA, your monthly payment will be permanently reduced—by as much as 25% or 30%. Ouch. That is a dramatic drop in benefit amounts. So, you have to ask yourself, "Can I really afford to give up 1/3 of my monthly Social Security paycheck?" Most of us would answer, "No!" to that question.

Now, let's talk about the good news. If you wait to claim your Social Security benefits until after reaching your FRA, you get a "bonus." Your benefit will grow by 8% each year until you turn 70. This bonus money is called Delayed Retirement Credits (DRC), and your monthly benefit will go up each month you delay claiming after FRA until age 70.

Wage adjustments make a difference

You'll remember that Social Security calculates retirement benefits based on one's highest 35 years of wage history. But how does the income from the 1970s and 1980s compare to current wages? How can wages from decades ago be fairly used to determine a benefit today? Good question.

To calculate your personal benefit, Social Security considers your entire wage history. However, the dollars you earned early in your career are not directly used. Instead, each year's wages are adjusted by a specific factor that is "actuarially equivalent" to the value of the dollar in the year you turn 60. Any wages earned from age 60 onward are used as is, while all previous years' earnings are adjusted upward using a wage inflation index factor. This process makes all the years of work history more comparable.

Once the wage inflation factor has been applied, your highest 35 years of indexed wages will be used to calculate your personal benefit. These top 35 years of wages are summed up, then divided by 35 and further divided by 12 months to determine your Average Indexed Monthly Earnings (AIME). AIME represents the average monthly earnings over your entire work history.

An example of calculating AIME

Let's say that, after adjusting 45 years of work history for wage inflation, you select the highest 35 years and total them. For example, the total might be $2,950,800. Many people with long careers will find their total inflation-adjusted earnings exceed $1 million.

Here's how to calculate average indexed monthly earnings (AIME):

- ($2,950,800 total indexed wages) / (35 years) = $84,309 average annual wages / (12 months per year) = $7,026 per month

Here's where the math starts to really kick in. AIME is the first step in calculating your insurance benefit. It is not the amount of your social insurance payment.

Calculating a Primary Insurance Amount—PIA

Your AIME now gets split into three tiers to calculate your Primary Insurance Amount (PIA). These tiers, or bands, are determined by the actuaries and updated each year. If you turn 62 in 2025, these are your tiers:

- 90% of the first $1,226 of your AIME
- 32% of AIME that falls between $1,226 and $7,391
- 15% of any remaining AIME over $7,391

Returning to the example above, for the person with an AIME of $7,026, the PIA is approximately $2,959. If their AIME were $3,500 instead, the calculated PIA would be about $1,830. And for someone who has been earning at or above the taxable wage base ($176,100 in 2025) throughout most of their career, they will have a PIA that maxes out at over $4,000 per month. Table 1 shows the calculations for each of these examples:

TABLE 1

	2025 Parameters	AIME = $7,026	AIME = $3,500	AIME = $14,000
1ˢᵗ Tier	90% of $1,226	$1,103	$1,103	$1,103
2ⁿᵈ Tier	32% of AIME between $7,391 and $1,226	$1,856	$727	$1,973
3ʳᵈ Tier	15% of AIME above $7,391	n/a	n/a	$991
Primary Insurance Amount		$2,959	$1,831	$4,067

This is the basic idea behind calculating Social Security's insurance benefit. The calculations are squarely focused on fairness based on your own eligibility (you earned 40 credits or more) and your unique work journey and wage record (your highest 35 years). The rest is just some math.

When your money is not really your money

You pay real dollars into Social Security when working for a covered employer. In exchange, you receive a calculated benefit payment throughout retirement. The money you contribute while working is used to pay benefits for current retirees.

It is important to remember a key concept behind Social Security: it was not established as a welfare program. It was designed as a self-funding system where workers pay in now to receive benefits later. By earning credits through participation during your work years, you'll qualify for benefits later in retirement. It's a promise across generations that has successfully delivered for 90 years and counting.

Paying your fair share

The money that comes out of each paycheck isn't specifically set aside for you. The fact that you're contributing your share acts as credits, or "chits in the bank," for your future benefits.

Sometimes people get frustrated by that fact. "I paid in tens of thousands of dollars over my career! Why can't I get all of that back? It is my money!" No, it's not. And it never was.

Here's how to look at your share that gets paid into Social Security. Anyone who lives a long time in retirement will get back their original contributions plus a whole lot more, including annual increases to help offset inflation. They also provide benefits for their spouse, ex-spouse, and surviving spouse if the higher-earning spouse or ex-spouse dies. Your contributions to Social Security also cover minor children if a parent is older and qualifies for Social Security or if the parent dies. And there's more.

In fact, those who live 30 years in retirement can receive as much as two and a half times more than the contributions they and their employers made.

A simple example illustrates the power of the program

Keeping in mind that my example is not an exact calculation and is only meant only to illustrate the power of the Social

Security program, here are some rough figures to show the advantage of Social Security retirement benefits.

- Assume you worked for 45 years for a covered employer and met the taxable wage base each year. Your first job was in 1980, and your last paycheck was at the end of 2024.

- You would have paid about $231,000 into Social Security, not adjusted for inflation.

- Your employer would have paid in roughly the same amount, or slightly higher. That's another $231,000.

- Contributions made into Social Security on your behalf would total about $462,000.

Now, let's adjust for inflation using Social Security's index inflation factors from 1980 to 2024. In 2024 dollars, you've paid just under $400,000 into Social Security, and your employer has matched that amount, totaling $800,000 in inflation-adjusted dollars.

Any way you look at these numbers, they are large. This is a significant amount of money being contributed to the program by you and your employer(s), and in turn, paid out to current recipients of Social Security, including your parents, grandparents, and many others you love.

Living many years in retirement

Let's assume you live 30 years in retirement, from age 67 to 97. This is a realistic possibility for many people. Women generally have higher odds of reaching very advanced ages, but many men will also be in this club. Every month during your 30-year retirement, you will receive a Social Security payment – no questions asked.

Assuming you earned at the taxable wage base every year, your highest 35 years of earnings yield a PIA of about $4,000.

After 30 years, you'll have received just shy of $2.1 million! (That's using a straight-line annual inflation factor of 2.5%).

So, you and your employer paid in roughly $800,000, and yet you receive $2.1 million in benefits. That's over two and a half times the amount that was contributed on your behalf.

What if you only live 25 years in retirement? Then your benefits would total about $1.6 million, which is twice the amount contributed on your behalf.

This is the power behind our Social Security insurance program. And this one, in particular, is remarkable in that it insures you if you live a long life. You'll "recoup" your $200,000 in contributions after just 4 ½ years into retirement, and the full amount contributed on your behalf (by you and your employer) is returned to you in about 8 ½ years.

Anyone who has earned a high income throughout their career and reaches about age 78 has been repaid, if you want to look at it that way. And those who are in their late 80s, 90s, or 100s... well, that's one heck of a good deal on their insurance policy!

The only problem here is that you have no way of knowing if you'll live to a ripe old age. That's why it's called insurance.

Bottom line: Social Security is a 90-year success story...and it continues

Things regarding Social Security are more uncertain today in 2025 than they have been since the late 1970s. Many of you were still in high school or college back then. Definitely not worried about retirement! Some of you reading this book weren't even born yet.

While there is uncertainty and the projections from the actuaries show that the reserve account will be fully tapped and spent by early 2033, this insurance program is too important to be dismantled. Congress just needs to get its act together to implement some of the dozens of proposals that have been suggested over the last 25 years.

Meanwhile, for anyone 50 and older, you should confidently expect to receive a payment every month during your retirement. Your spouse will also receive a steady check throughout their retirement. For those younger, well, the program is less certain. I believe there will continue to be a strong social safety net. However, some changes are needed to strengthen the program, ensuring retirees get the benefits they were promised. How Social Security will adapt to meet future obligations is still undecided, but many good and viable options are available.

Most importantly, we learn something very valuable from the 80- and 90-year-olds who have been receiving Social Security for 20 or more years. They will tell you it's a darn good thing to be getting these insurance payments.

Consider the following: A large number of elderly Social Security beneficiaries depend on Social Security for at least half of their total income. For those families and individuals 65 and older, we find:

- For half of retirees, 50% or more of their family income comes from Social Security, while about a quarter of retired families rely on Social Security for 90% or more of their income.

- Approximately 45% of retired men report that 50% or more of their income comes from Social Security, while 53% of retired women report that at least half of their income comes from Social Security.[7]

One of the core tenets of the Social Security Act of 1935 was to keep America's elderly out of poverty. The program was not designed to provide former workers and their spouses with great riches. It was intended to keep food on the table during old age. In that sense, Social Security has been a wildly success-ful program for 90 years and remains so today. Frankly, very few Americans could make it through retirement without this critical social insurance program in place. Would you?

CHAPTER 7:

How Much Do You Really Need to Know?

It is important to understand key elements of the Social Security program. No, you don't need to be a math whiz. In fact, if you just download your statement and review your numbers, that will be enough for most planning needs. The calculations have already been done based on your actual wage history.

What you need to understand are some facts about the program and how your personal work history can impact your retirement income. The more you understand the more confident you'll be in making the best decisions before claiming your benefit. Additionally, tracking your progress over time allows you to see how your benefit estimate increases or decreases as your wages change.

One lady I met carried a retirement countdown clock on her smartphone. She had a demanding, stressful job and could hardly wait to retire. She knew she wanted to claim benefits at her Full Retirement Age, but it would be hard to wait that long. She found a "countdown to retirement" app that motivated her to stay on the job. Even though more than 700 days remained until retirement, it made her happy to watch the daily countdown: 732 days, 8 hours, 41 minutes, 06 seconds. It really was this exact.

Ten important factors to consider before claiming your benefit

1. **Your monthly check will be reduced significantly if you claim at 62:** Up to a whopping 30%. Is it worth claiming early if you're going to lock in permanently lower income? You might not have a choice, or you could have plenty of other money. But, it's important to understand the implications and consequences of claiming so early. You don't want to regret this decision when you're 85.

2. **Your own work history drives your benefit amount.** If you were fortunate enough to earn a lot of money during your career, that's great. The maximum Social Security payout was just over $2,800 per month if you reached FRA in 2019, and it's up to $4,000 per month if you reached FRA in 2025. Ah, the effect of high inflation and rising wages. If your career paid less, you would receive a benefit based on those earnings.

3. **You need 40 credits to qualify.** Don't stop working if you have 36 credits and want to claim on your own work record. You need 40 credits to receive your own benefits. (Generally, that means working for 10 years and paying a minimum amount of FICA on a certain amount of income.)

4. **The maximum number of credits you can earn is four per year.** In 2025, you must earn at least $7,240 from covered employment to receive four credits.

5. **Don't worry if you have moved in and out of the workforce.** Many people come in and out of paid work during a 40-to-50-year career. This is more common among women, but an increasing number of men now take time off as well. Social Security only counts your your highest 35 years of earnings. These don't have to

be consecutive years. However, if you have fewer than 35 years of earnings, zeros will be included.

6. **Social Security classifies you into one of four categories:** an individual worker, a spouse, an ex-spouse, or a surviving spouse/ex-spouse. You are considered in only one of these categories when you claim your benefits. Throughout your life, you may move in and out of all four categories.

7. **You can only receive one benefit at a time, and it will be the highest benefit available to you when you file.** If you are an individual worker and spouse, you'll receive one benefit check, which will be from the category that provides the most money per month.

8. **If you are in a same-sex marriage, the same benefits and rules apply.** Married is married from Social Security's perspective. If you have a legal marriage or a qualifying common-law marriage, you are eligible to claim spousal benefits, ex-spouse benefits, or surviving spouse/ex-spouse benefits if they increase your own benefit payment. You will receive one benefit at a time, and it will be the highest one for which you are eligible.

9. **If you can wait to claim until after your FRA, you'll boost your monthly benefit.** Those who wait can increase their monthly income by as much as 24% or 32%. However, you need a solid plan to take advantage of this, which often involves working until age 70 or having substantial savings to retire comfortably before claiming Social Security.

10. **Staking your claim is all but irrevocable.** There are only a couple of ways to undo your claim. You'll have to pay back all the money you've received from Social Security or stop payments for several years. These

options usually don't work for most people. Be very careful when making your claim. Make sure you really want to start receiving those benefits before you push the button.

Start with SSA.gov to look for your situation and options

It can take some time to understand how your specific benefit will work. This is especially true if you've been married multiple times. Before you consider claiming, do some additional research about your situation and spend time on www.SSA.gov.

If you have any kind of special circumstances, you'll likely find information on www.SSA.gov to address your situation, including:

- If you want to remarry after your spouse dies, what are the implications for your surviving spouse benefits?

- If your spouse has been or is currently incarcerated, how does that affect your benefits?

- What if you are a disabled military veteran?

- If your spouse is considerably older than you and is retiring, and you have children together, are there benefits for the children?

- Have you been a victim of domestic violence? There are special rules that can assist you in applying for a new Social Security Number.

Use www.SSA.gov as your go-to resource. Sometimes, life can get pretty messy. Use this website to find information, phone numbers, or field offices where you can confidentially discuss your situation with an agent.

SECTION 2
Four Social Security Claiming Categories

Social security has four claiming categories based on your marital status when you claim: you will be an individual worker, a spouse, an ex-spouse, or a surviving spouse or ex-spouse.

Find the section that matches your category. Review the general rules and examples of real people in the same category.

SECTION 2A
Information If You Are Single

CHAPTER 8:

Social Security for Individual Workers

When you think about the era when the Social Security Act was created—90 years ago—America looked very different from how it does now. The country was relatively new in its industrial strength. Family farms were still functioning as family farms. Child labor laws were just beginning to be enforced. We had emerged from a world war, started manufacturing automobiles in large numbers, and finally began to recover from the crippling Great Depression.

During the early 1900s, families began to spread out over miles and generations for the first time. However, the tradition of men and women marrying and having children continued. As did the traditional household division of labor and roles. The husband worked outside the home for wages, more often in factories, while the wife managed the household and raised the children.

But in this system, there was no one to care for the elderly who could no longer work. Over half of the elderly lived in poverty.

Enter Social Security as a program for workers

With this new economic and family structure in place, Franklin Delano Roosevelt's administration came into power. One of the first major pieces of legislation passed during his presidency was Social Security. At the heart of this social insurance program was providing retirement benefits to workers when they reached old age (defined as age 65). It wasn't a program limited to male workers or white workers; it was simply intended to provide benefits to workers at companies.

The fact of the matter, however, was that it was mostly men who initially met the work requirements. But during World War II, millions of women found themselves working long hours in factories, offices, and other jobs provided by large employers. All in support of the war effort. Women were not only filling a critical role while men were deployed, but they were also gaining a new sense of their own value.

For the first time, large numbers of women earned income, and their wages included future retirement benefits. Like any worker, FICA taxes were deducted from their paychecks, and they accumulated credits. The main difference, of course, was that women's wages were much lower than those of men, resulting in significantly reduced retirement benefits. This issue still exists today. However, it's worth noting that including women as recipients of Social Security from the start is truly remarkable.

The 1940s marked a significant turning point in women's financial independence. If they worked long enough to earn their 40 credits, they would qualify for Social Security retirement benefits as individual workers, not just as a spouse.

By the end of the Great Depression, some 11 million women, or 25% of women ages 14 and older, were earning wages. Many worked in factories producing garments, candy, or automobile parts. Some were schoolteachers, others nurses, and some secretaries. Three out of ten worked as domestic housekeepers or in personal service roles. In rural areas, women tended to the family farms.[8]

Wages offered to women were significantly lower than those for men. In 1937, women's average annual pay was $525, compared to over $1,027 for men. Women were often ridiculed for taking jobs outside the home. Society generally believed that for every job a woman took, a man was cheated out of it. However, employers were happy to hire women at much lower salaries, and women were willing to accept the jobs and lower wages that most men refused.

The individual worker's benefit

And so, as the Social Security program progressed, it included more workers and more future beneficiaries participating in the system. The Social Security law is highly prescriptive in how each individual worker can receive a retirement benefit. Each individual must meet the general rules:

- Earned 40 credits.

- Worked for a covered employer.

- Attained retirement age – originally 65, then later 62 for reduced benefits.

The old-age insurance benefit, called the Primary Insurance Amount (PIA), is calculated the same way for all workers. An individual, or "single," worker is someone who falls into any of these groups:

- Not currently married, or never married.

- Married, but has accrued at least 40 credits on their own work record.

- Not a qualifying divorced person – defined as someone who was not married for 10 years or longer before a divorce.

- A widow or widower with their own 40 Social Security credits.

Individuals become eligible for Social Security as early as age 62. However, claiming benefits that early comes with a steep penalty—up to a 30% permanent reduction in monthly income. They also have the option to wait until their Full Retirement Age (FRA) to claim, or as late as age 70. Those who wait to claim after FRA and up to age 70 receive a "bonus" of 8% more per year. This permanent increase is allocated at a monthly rate of .667% (8% divided by 12 months).

In this section of the book, the focus is on individuals who file taxes as single filers. We'll first cover individuals because they bear the full responsibility for their Social Security decisions. There's no other record to consider. So their claiming decision carries significant weight.

If you are married or a qualified divorced individual, you will have two benefit calculations to review but will only receive the higher one. Married couples and divorced individuals are covered in the following sections.

Solo responsibility for retirement

As of 2023, nearly 92 million people age 25 and older in the U.S. were unmarried. About 56% had never married, and the remaining 44% either divorced or widowed.[9]

By age 65, the picture looks quite different. There are approximately 7.4 million single men and 15.5 million single women. And the number of widows outpaces the number of widowers 3-to-1.[10] They can often rely on survivor benefits, but many divorced individuals and all those who never married are on their own to create sufficient retirement income. Social Security is an essential piece to their financial security, so when to claim is a critical decision.

There are many factors to consider when thinking about Social Security retirement benefits as a solo individual, including:

- how much you have in other retirement savings accounts,
- what your housing arrangement will be in retirement,

- how much debt you are managing as you approach retirement,

- how healthy you are, and

- what you will do with your time when you stop working.

You'll want to weigh the importance of maximizing your benefits from Social Security. Even during times when it seems there are insurmountable problems with Social Security's funding, Congress will eventually take action. However, they are clearly in no rush to do so. You, on the other hand, are stuck with whatever decision you make.

The solid foundation Social Security will provide for your income in old age is simply too important to leave to chance, and taking the time to educate yourself about the implications of your decision is an all-important step.

Social Security decisions are top of mind for individuals

Talking with single people is impressive. They are clearly knowledgeable about their retirement income options, especially Social Security. They are thoughtful and deeply aware of their self-reliance and financial situation. Unless faced with external circumstances like caring for an aging parent or unexpectedly losing a job, most single individuals plan to work longer, continue saving for retirement, and enjoy all that friends and family offer.

Often, single people take pride in their nieces and nephews, who are important parts of their lives. They want to help with college expenses or ensure they leave a legacy. Others find fulfillment in volunteer work and plan to leave parts of their estates to charities that matter to them. Whatever way they choose to direct their assets, more money is better than less.

Achieving their important goals requires making strategic decisions about when to claim Social Security.

Meet two single women making smart choices about Social Security

In the next two chapters, you'll get a glimpse into the lives of two single women who took control of their financial futures. I would have included a scenario for a single man, but it turns out all the single men I once knew ended up getting married— either to a woman or, after same-sex marriages became legal in all the states, to their long-time partners.

This isn't to say there aren't plenty of single men out there... there are just a lot fewer of them, and they haven't reached out to me to discuss their Social Security planning.

- Jane – Married for nine years, she does not qualify for ex-spouse benefits. She's learned to make smart decisions about her work and retirement benefits.

- Karen – A single lady her entire life, she's built a successful career and a small business. She wouldn't trade a thing. Now that she's nearing retirement age, she's all business with her money.

Download your free action plan and checklist on my blog, Boomer Retirement Briefs at https://boomerretirementbriefs.com.

CHAPTER 9:

Making It On Your Own, Even Though Once Married

Jane recalls her wonderful childhood growing up in the South, marching in her high school band, falling in love with, and marrying her high school boyfriend. He was a free spirit, and they wanted an outdoor life. They moved out West and started a family. They had five children (including two sets of twins) in short order, and she loved being a stay-at-home mom during those years. Her husband never held a steady job; he did just enough odd jobs to cover the basics.

The marriage didn't last. After five years, Jane realized things weren't going well, but they tried to keep it together. They were young and had responsibilities for their growing children. After eight years, they filed for divorce. It was finalized just after their ninth anniversary.

It was an amicable divorce, and the two stayed friends over the years. They stayed out West, raising the children together and taking on odd jobs to make ends meet. Jane loved growing her own vegetables and cooking with the kids. She found joy in the everyday things.

Time for a fresh start

After the kids were grown and launched, Jane moved back to her hometown. She's working hard to earn her own way. She's starting to piece things together to stay afloat financially and save for the future. Jane has no regrets about her early lifestyle, but she wishes she had known the importance of making enough to earn 40 credits for her Social Security benefits.

Now, as she and her ex-husband are nearing age 65, it turns out he doesn't qualify for Social Security on his own record. Jane hasn't earned enough for 40 quarters to qualify for her own benefit yet, but she is close. When reviewing her irregular work history, she can see that most of her years of earnings were not considered substantial. She now sees the downside of jobs where she was paid in cash without any withholdings for Social Security. Her benefit amount is truly modest. She's working full-time now and plans to keep working until her mid-70s if she can.

Qualifying on your own record

Jane was initially worried she wouldn't qualify for Social Security at all. She asked, "Is there any way to get Social Security when your husband never worked enough to earn his 40 quarters? A lot of his pay was 'under the table' and he didn't work for big companies."

It turns out that isn't an issue for Jane. Because she and her ex weren't married for the required 10 years or longer, neither of them can use each other's work record to claim ex-spousal benefits. The good news is Jane will qualify for Social Security retirement benefits based on her own work record.

Jane is hardly alone in discovering her ex-husband does not qualify for Social Security – and that they weren't married long enough for her to claim benefits on him anyway. Many divorced women only find out at retirement that their ex-spouses aren't eligible for Social Security. And find themselves approaching retirement without a social safety net.

Time to figure out your options

As Jane figured out, it's going to be critical for her to keep working and earning credits so she can qualify for Social Security benefits. She wanted to be sure she was on track to earn her 40 credits, despite her inconsistent work history. Luckily, Social Security doesn't care when you earn your credits; as long as you reach a total of 40, you qualify.

At age 65, she has accumulated 36 credits. Just four more quarters of work, and she will qualify to collect Social Security retirement benefits as an individual worker.

Jane looks much younger than her 65 years. She says she feels great and plans to keep working as long as she can. She doesn't earn a high hourly wage, so every dollar really matters. She'd like to find a new job with higher wages. Even earning just two or three additional dollars an hour would increase her wages enough to impact the highest 35 years of earnings used in her benefit calculation.

It's a good plan for her to keep working as long as possible. Not only do these earnings increase her Social Security payments, but if she waits until age 70 to claim, she will have earned all her delayed retirement credits, boosting her monthly benefit by 32%.

Illustrating Jane's possible outcomes

Social Security income will be very important for any woman in a situation like Jane's. It is essential for her to do everything she can to qualify for retirement benefits and then boost them by continuing to work at a higher-wage job.

Her current Primary Insurance Amount (PIA) is estimated at $1,150 per month. If she continues working and delays claiming until age 70, her benefit jumps to $1,550 per month.

Furthermore, she can continue working after age 70. Social Security will recalculate her benefits each year she earns income.

When you have 20 or more years of zeros on your work record, replacing even a few of those years makes a difference. Combining the extra years of work with delayed retirement credits can make a tremendous difference.

Summary

Jane mentioned that it was a little hard to swallow that she now has to create her own retirement after spending her early years as a wife and mother, and later as a single mother. Despite her situation, she remains in high spirits. Moving back to her hometown, reconnecting with extended family and old friends from high school, and finding a job she enjoys turned out to be the right move for her. Overall, she's really enjoying her late 60s.

As a single woman with gaps in work history, it's important to remember key facts when planning for Social Security income.

- You'll have to earn 40 quarters on your own work record to qualify for retirement benefits.

- You'll need to rely solely on your own earnings for the calculated benefit. Social Security will determine your benefit based on your highest 35 years of wages, including any zeros. The more zeros you can replace, the higher your monthly income will be.

- In very few cases, you might qualify for a minimum Social Security payment depending on the total years of covered employment.

- Your full retirement benefit becomes available the month of your FRA.

- If you can wait to claim until age 70, you will receive

your maximum benefit, which includes increases of 8% per year from "Delayed Retirement Credits".

• Even after reaching age 70, you can continue to work. Your benefit will be recalculated each year, and the result is likely to increase benefits by replacing another zero with current income and then applying annual cost-of-living adjustments.

CHAPTER 10:

A Life-Long Single Lady Who Wouldn't Change a Thing

Karen begins the conversation with, "65! Incredulous! How did this happen to me?" Karen is a dynamo — a remarkable woman full of life, energy, and endless enthusiasm for last-minute adventures. She's a technology guru and website developer who has been running her own small business for over 20 years. She loves her work, and her clients adore her. She's been an independent spirit for as long as she can remember, and although she dated here and there over the years, marriage or settling down was never important to her. She is fiercely independent and loves the life she has built as a single woman.

Sporting heritage red hair and an Irish background, Karen decided to study Spanish in college in the mid-1970s. She spent time in Spain, where her love of travel was born. Her career started back in high school, this time as a Spanish teacher. Although rewarding, it didn't pay particularly well. When a friend suggested she join a large computer company in 1983, she decided to make the leap. She entered the tech sector just as it was experiencing its meteoric rise. She advanced in the organization through various roles in technology, operations, and project management. In 1997, the tech giant went bankrupt.

Karen was out of a job during her prime earning years. Now what? She saw her situation as an opportunity and decided to start her own business. What did she have to lose? For the past 20-something years, it's been all good.

Along the way, Karen has focused on a few key financial tactics. She admits she's not a financial expert but is savvy enough to know that she owns her financial present and future. Decades ago, she bought a house within her budget, and it is now fully paid off. She felt it was important to own that roof over her head outright, and well before she retired. Karen has been saving small amounts of money—pennies, nickels, and dimes—in various retirement accounts over the years. The 401(k) she contributed to during her big-company days remains invested for her future. "Drive slow and steady" is her philosophy, so there's been no need for fancy, fast, or expensive cars.

Turning 65 and going strong

For her 65th birthday, she chose a long weekend in Las Vegas with a close friend. Her large circle of friends complained, wanting to celebrate with a big party. Karen wasn't budging. "You aren't the boss of me! I'm going to Vegas my way for my birthday," she told her friends. She watched the solar eclipse and was enchanted by Celine Dion at her Caesar's Palace concert.

Although she didn't accept her friends' idea for a birthday party, Karen has realized how important it is for single women to have a close circle of friends and listen to their experiences and insights. One of the most valuable things she's learned from older friends is that Social Security income is not nearly enough. This isn't something people often think about when preparing to retire. Only then does one find out it's designed to replace about 40% of income, and that's only if you were a middle-income worker. It's not meant to cover all expenses in retirement, but when that first check arrives and you see how small it is, it's quite a shock.

Knowing that crucial fact has directly influenced Karen's financial outlook. She has downloaded her Social Security statement and has been reviewing it. Assuming all goes well for her and her business, she's planned to work until age 71 ½. That's a pretty specific age. Was there a reason?

Confusion between Social Security's age 70 and the IRS's age 70 ½

Many people who aren't experts in tax law or accounting often get confused by complex retirement rules. Karen had heard that 71 ½ is an important age—it's when she can maximize Social Security and must start withdrawing money from her IRAs. Since her retirement income depends entirely on her, she wants to ensure she's maximizing every dollar.

She was thrilled to learn that her dates were slightly off. She could, in fact, retire 18 months earlier than she thought! It was a great day when she found this out. Since there's a lot of confusion about ages and dates, let's clarify:

For Social Security, your maximum payment occurs the month you turn 70. If you do not claim your benefit at 70, you might leave some of your money on the table. Social Security will pay you a retroactive six-month lump sum when you claim if you are older than Full Retirement Age and could have claimed six months earlier. If Karen waits until 71 ½ to make her first claim, she would miss out on 12 months of income that was rightfully hers.

Karen can continue working well past 70 if she chooses. She would still claim her Social Security at 70. Each year afterward, if she has income, Social Security will review her benefit calculation to see if she can receive a larger benefit by including her current year's earnings.

Now she's clear on the maximum Social Security claiming age. It's 70.

Required Minimum Distribution (RMD) ages have changed

For decades, the IRS has required IRA and retirement plan owners to start withdrawing money at age 70½. This is known as RMD, or Required Minimum Distributions. However, since 2020, during the COVID-19 pandemic, two important laws were passed that significantly changed these retirement RMD rules.

- In the Setting Every Community Up for Retirement Security, SECURE 1.0, the RMD age was changed to 72, starting in 2020.

- Then, in 2022, SECURE 2.0 was enacted, and the RMD age was changed again. This time, it became 73 for some people (generally those born from 1952 to 1959) and 75 for those born after 1959. Additionally, the 50% penalty for missing an RMD was reduced to 25% and may be 10% in some situations.

RMD rules specify how much you must withdraw from any and all traditional IRAs, employer-sponsored retirement plans, and small business retirement accounts. A specific calculation determines the withdrawal amount for each account, which is reported as income on your tax returns. If you fail to meet the minimum distribution requirement, you may face a tax penalty.

Karen was learning about all of this and was very happy to discover she can delay taking distributions and paying taxes on her IRA assets.

There is an exception to the RMD rule: If you continue working for an employer after reaching your RMD age, you are not required to withdraw any amount from that employer's 401(k) or 403(b) plan until you retire, unless you are an owner of the company.

So, in Karen's case, as a small business owner, she cannot delay starting her RMDs. But the starting line moved from 70 ½ to 73.

You can see that the rules are complicated, and there are many opportunities for mistakes. A small misunderstanding on Karen's part ended up being good news for her. She won't leave any Social Security benefits on the table. Phew! She can wait a few more years before she needs to start tapping into her IRA. And she can retire a full year earlier than she thought possible. She might not choose to, but knowing she has the option was unexpectedly good news for her.

The numbers are meaningful

Karen is planning carefully and working hard to maximize her income for a long retirement. She's fairly certain she'll need to stop traveling at some point, probably in her mid-80s, but she'll still require a good amount of money to reach 100.

Let's assume Karen's successful career started at age 22. At 65, she's got a robust work history of 43 years. She will have 48 years of earnings if she continues working until age 70. When she checked her Social Security statement, she noticed four years of missing earnings. She had zeroes from 1979–1982, which were the years she was teaching. Instead of Social Security contributions, her employer sponsored a pension plan. That was a surprise to Karen. She's wondering if she will be entitled to any pension payments now that she's 65. She will need to call the state teacher's union. Maybe she'll receive a small amount if she met the minimum years for eligibility.

Otherwise, she has maintained a continuous and mostly increasing work history. Her highest 35 years of earnings will come from her most recent years. With a strong income record, Karen's numbers might look like this:

- If she works until her FRA of 66, her monthly benefit, or Primary Insurance Amount, would be $2,532.

- If she keeps working until age 70 before claiming, she'll earn the 8% per year delayed retirement credit "bonus," and her monthly payments will permanently increase to about $3,340.

The bonus will provide her with more than $800 in guaranteed monthly income for her entire retirement. You can see what a powerful decision it is to wait before claiming, especially when you must rely only on your own income and resources. If Karen can wait until age 70, she will position herself in the most financially secure way possible.

And the more Karen can pull in from Social Security, the less she'll need to use her own savings beyond the minimum required. That will give her greater flexibility to travel whenever she wants, and to all the places she wants to go.

Summary

Women who have always been single tend to have a clear understanding of their financial picture. They are realistic about their abilities and the consequences of their decisions. Not all women are as skilled at managing their finances as Karen has been, but their level of financial awareness is impressive.

Some single women will want to keep working because it lets them delay using their personal savings. Others want to retire early and start a new chapter. The key step is to take some time to evaluate all your personal resources and create a plan you're comfortable with. Keep in mind you may spend a long time in retirement.

Listen to the advice of single women who have already claimed Social Security. The income might not be as high as you'd like, so choose your starting date carefully.

SECTION 2B

The Basics for Happily Married Couples

Married Couples – Coordinating Benefits and Claiming Decisions

Ah, marriage. Isn't it grand? I ask audiences across the country to raise their hands if they are part of a happily married couple. There are bursts of laughter. A few hands go up immediately, and many wives elbow their husbands, loudly whispering, "Raise your hand! We are happily married!" It energizes the crowd and keeps them interested in what could otherwise be a daunting topic: Social Security benefits for married couples.

This section of the book includes several examples of how spouses at different ages and in various situations need to consider their claiming strategies and the timing of their claims. You can find a detailed checklist and action plan for married couples on my Boomer Retirement Briefs blog at https://boomerretirementbriefs.com.

First, let's review the general rules for married couples. This will give you a solid foundation on how Social Security works for married couples before diving into specific scenarios.

Recognizing homemakers and mothers

One of the most notable features of the Social Security retirement program is that, almost from the start, the law's architects recognized the role of the married woman. Looking back to the 1930s, that was a quite progressive idea. Social Security clearly acknowledged a wife's role in the household and that she deserved her own paycheck in retirement. That women only receive half of their husbands' benefit amounts... well, that could have been more generous!

The reason for at-home moms and homemakers to receive a paycheck comes from recognizing that it was the couple – the happily married couple – who together created a successful economic unit. If Mom wasn't home caring for the children, then Dad wouldn't be able to work, produce, and support the family. It was the strength of the partnership that fueled the country's economic engine, each contributing in their own way. When they retired, Congress acknowledged that both had been working all along — one outside the home, the other inside it.

The basic rules for spouses

Starting in the 1930s, understanding benefits for married couples generally assumed the husband was the breadwinner and the wife the homemaker, with no outside income. There was no recognition of partners at that time, or same-sex marriages or relationships.

When the husband turned 65, he retired and began collecting Social Security. At that time, his non-wage-earning wife became eligible for a retirement benefit once she reached age 65. (It wasn't until 1956 that women could claim early at age 62; and not until 1961 for men to claim early.) She would receive 50% of his Primary Insurance Amount (PIA) when she turned 65, or she would get a reduced payment if she claimed earlier.

If a husband was entitled to $500 per month at his Full Retirement Age (FRA) of 65, his wife was entitled to $250 per month once she turned 65. The total household income would be $750. Back in the 1940s and 1950s, implementing spousal benefits was relatively simple and straightforward.

A turning point for wives: World War II

In December 1941, the United States entered World War II. Women were asked to manage their households and take on jobs for the war effort. It turns out that this single request – for more women to join the workforce – set the stage for increased complexity in Social Security. This was an unintended consequence.

When women started working outside the home, they discovered they were capable, valued on the job, and empowered to influence the household's financial success. By the time they reached retirement age of 65 in the 1970s and 1980s, many had worked long enough to earn the 40 required credits. These women, who supported the war effort through their work, now qualified for their own retirement benefits. They also qualified for spousal benefits, and things got interesting. From Social Security's perspective, married women now fell into several possible sub-categories.

In what I call the original role, some wives worked only temporarily, on an as-needed basis. Some helped support the war effort. Others worked for a few years before getting married, or occasionally to cover household bills or extras. Over the years, they didn't earn 40 credits. They weren't eligible for Social Security benefits based on their own record, but they did qualify as spouses. This group of women would receive half of their husband's PIA when they turned 65. If he got $800 at age 65, she received $400. Simple and straightforward.

Then, there was the "emerging" group of semi-independent wives who worked outside the home long enough to earn their 40 credits. So, on their own, they independently qualified for their individual worker retirement benefits AND spousal benefits. But would they receive their own benefit, their spousal benefit, or both?

There is no "double dipping" when it comes to Social Security, so they weren't going to get both benefits. The rules state that when you are eligible for two benefits at the same time, you receive only one – the higher one. In the case of this group of wives, their benefits consist of two parts: their own worker benefit plus a spousal top-up benefit. To illustrate:

- Assume a wife has her own PIA of $500 per month and a calculated spousal benefit of $800 per month.

- Her maximum calculated value is $800, which is the highest amount she can receive at her FRA.

- However, her maximum benefit is paid in two parts: she will receive her own $500 from her work record, plus a spousal "top up" of $300. The combined payments bring her to her highest calculated benefit.

Now, assume a wife is eligible for a monthly benefit of $950 based on her own work record, and her calculated spousal benefit is $800 per month. What happens next? Again, she'll receive the highest of the benefits she's eligible for. In this case, the husband still earns more than his wife. (His PIA is $1,600 per month.) However, her own work record is high enough that she isn't entitled to any spousal top-up. Therefore, she will receive $950 per month, based on her own work record, if she claims at her FRA.

In this evolution of women's work history, in recent years, we know that some wives have earned more than their husbands. Let's assume a wife has a monthly benefit at her FRA of $3,400. Her husband, who also had a good career, has a calculated benefit of $3,000 per month. Now, Social Security will review both spouses' situations and determine which benefits apply to whom.

- Her calculated spousal benefit would be half of his PIA, or $1,500, so she will not receive this lower spousal benefit.

- Her benefit will be her own $3,400 per month at her FRA.

- His spousal benefit would be half of her PIA, or $1,700. He is not eligible for the lower spousal benefit.

- His best benefit will be his own $3,000 per month at his FRA.

- In this case, each spouse's maximum benefit is based on their own work history. Neither qualifies for spousal benefits. Overall, their household income will be $6,400 per month if both claim at their FRA.

- Either or both could also wait to claim after FRA and earn some Delayed Retirement Credits. By waiting, they may build a stronger foundation for their retirement income.

Today, Social Security doesn't consider who the higher earner is or if you receive more from your spousal benefit or your own record. The key factors for a couple are:

- There is either a higher earner and a lower earner, or two earners with equal income.

- Both members of the couple are eligible for a retirement paycheck.

- Each member of the couple is entitled to one benefit at a time, and it is the highest for which they are eligible.

Same-sex married couples are married in the eyes of Social Security

The Social Security spousal rules are also "spouse agnostic." This is an important factor for same-sex married couples. When the section of the Defense of Marriage Act that excluded same-sex couples from marrying was finally repealed in June 2015, same-sex spouses were immediately covered under Social Security's existing provisions. It was one small victory for those who had been fighting long and hard for the benefits of marriage equality.

Generally, to qualify for spousal benefits, couples must have been married to their current spouse for at least 12 months. However, same-sex couples who previously had civil or domestic partnerships because they couldn't legally marry might not need to wait an additional 12 months before starting to receive spousal payments. Their prior partnership could be recognized as qualifying time, allowing benefits to begin immediately. The SSA strongly advises older same-sex couples who are now married to apply for benefits promptly so they can determine if they are entitled to any back payments. This includes spousal benefits and any payments that might have been due to children or other eligible family members.

If you have questions about the benefits you can receive as a same-sex couple, read the information on www.SSA.gov. You might want to schedule an appointment at your local Social Security office or call for a consultation. There isn't a lot of information on Security's website for same-sex married couples, but it's a good place to start your research.

When you're eligible to claim benefits, and your situation is straightforward, you can apply for your own benefits or spousal benefits online at www.SSA.gov. Otherwise, you should schedule an appointment with your local field office.

Spousal benefits are hitched to the wage earner

If you have your own work record, you can file for your benefits when it fits best in your overall retirement income plan. However, you can only file for spousal benefits once your spouse is already claiming theirs. You and your spouse come as a package. Similar to filing taxes jointly, your spousal benefits are like being on a tandem bike—you both need to be on the bike and pedaling to move forward.

If your only benefit is the spousal benefit, you cannot claim spousal payments until your higher-earning spouse claims their benefit AND you have reached at least age 62. The same rule applies for a spousal top-up. You can apply for your own benefit as early as age 62, but you cannot receive a top-up until the higher-earning spouse later claims their benefit. No one receives their Social Security retirement benefits before age 62. (Surviving spouse benefits are a different matter, discussed in later chapters.)

Suppose your husband is three years older than you and you qualify for spousal benefits. If he waits until his Full Retirement Age (FRA) of 67 to claim benefits, you'll have to wait until you're 64 to claim your spousal benefits. If, on the other hand, he claims at 62, you won't be eligible for spousal benefits yet, since you're only 59. You will need to wait until you turn 62, three years later, to file for your spousal benefits.

Furthermore, you can wait until after your spouse claims their benefit before you file. Why? It's often a good idea to wait until your FRA to maximize your payment. Claiming early will permanently lower your benefit.

Spousal benefit examples

Let's look at several examples for Sally Snowflake and Richard Raine. They have been married for over 12 months. He was born in 1960, she in 1963. They each reach their FRA at age 67.

Sally does not qualify for her own worker's benefit. Instead, she will receive a spousal benefit. The maximum spousal benefit Sally can receive is 50% of Richard's PIA. She will only get this maximum if she waits until her FRA.

Here are several possible scenarios Sally and Richard might consider (all numbers are approximate):

Richard's Claiming Age	His Benefit Amount	Sally's Claiming Age	Her Benefit Amount	Comments
67	$3,180	67	$1,590	Each waits until FRA to claim; she has to wait three years after he claims.
62	$2,225	67	$1,590	Even though he claimed early, her benefit is based on his PIA if she waits to claim until her FRA.
67	$3,180	64	$1,190	They claim at the same time. She's younger than FRA and locks in a permanently reduced benefit.
65	$2,690	62	$1,030	Both want to retire early and claim early; both amounts are permanently reduced.
70	$4,080	67	$1,590	He claims at 70, so she must wait until he claims to claim her spousal benefit. Spousal benefits are based on the higher-earner's PIA, not their age 70 benefit.

What you see in these examples is how married couples should think about the timing of their claim in a coordinated way. If he waits to claim until his FRA, she cannot receive any Social Security retirement benefits until she is at least age 64. Maybe that works best for their plan. Perhaps they want to maximize their income, so they will both wait until their FRA or even until he reaches age 70 to claim. Deciding when to claim Social Security is not an isolated decision. It involves coordination between spouses and depends on what works best for their overall financial situation and their comprehensive retirement income plan.

Two main points for spouses to remember:

1. The lower-earning spouse receives only half of the higher-earning spouse's PIA. It doesn't matter when the wage earner begins collecting—before FRA, at FRA, or after FRA. The spouse's benefit calculation is still based on the higher wage earner's PIA.

2. Whenever either person in the couple claims early, that person receives a permanent reduction in their benefit amount. The reduction can be quite steep if they claim at age 62.

Topping up later

What if the lower-earning spouse has benefits based on their own work record and is eligible for a spousal "top-up"? In this situation, the lower earner can choose to claim any time from age 62 to 70 on their own work record. If the higher-earning spouse isn't already claiming benefits, the lower earner can only stake their claim on their own work record. Remember, to receive any spousal benefit, the other spouse must also be claiming. Think of it as the higher earner needing to jump into the pool first, then the dependent spouse jumps in afterward.

In addition, the spousal top-up only becomes available when that spouse claims their own benefit as well. So, a lower-earning spouse cannot claim just their spousal top-up at, say, age 65, then wait until age 70 to claim their own worker benefit that has increased with delayed retirement credits. Your own benefits are linked to a spousal top-up at the time you claim.

The timing for receiving the topped-up portion of spousal benefits depends on the decisions made by the higher-earning spouse. Once that spouse claims, the lower earner then becomes eligible to receive a top-up as the spousal benefit.

An example might clarify things. Let's revisit Sally and Richard in a different scenario. Sally was the lower-wage worker, and her own PIA is $800 compared to Richard's PIA of $2,400. Her spousal top-up will be half of his PIA minus her own benefit: $2,400/2 = $1,200 - $800 = $400.

- Sally reaches her FRA of 67 and decides to claim her own retirement benefit.

- When Sally claims, she will receive her own full retirement benefit of $800 per month. There are no reductions because she claimed at FRA.

- At the same time, her calculated spousal top-up is $400 per month. However, she cannot access the top-up yet since Richard has not claimed his benefits. Remember the tandem bike. In this scenario, Sally starts out riding her own bike.

- Richard needs to wait a few months until 70 to claim, as he is the higher earner.

- Three months later, Richard turns 70 and claims his maximum benefit. He gets on the tandem bike, and they both ride together.

- Sally's spousal top-up now becomes available. Her $800 per month continues to be paid, and she requests the additional $400 per month in top-up benefits. She ultimately receives her maximum possible benefit.

Meanwhile, Richard's $2,400 monthly benefit has increased by 8% per year since he waited until age 70 to claim. His benefit receives a 24% boost, making his monthly income much higher than his original PIA, to about $4,080. It will be even higher with annual COLAs in addition to the yearly 8% Delayed Retirement Credits, but you get the general concept here. Although Richard waited to maximize his benefit, Sally's spousal top-up is based on his original PIA. Her benefit does not increase based on his age-70 claim amount.

Sure, it's a little complicated here for spouses. Just remember, no one can receive a fully-loaded, topped-up spousal benefit until both are claiming.

Claiming early will cost you

One last important factor in the rules for spouses relates to when you apply for your benefit. Your FRA depends on the year you were born. Your PIA, or anchor, is calculated based on that year.

If you claim benefits at any month before reaching FRA, you will lock in a permanent reduction in your benefit. Permanent reductions apply whether you are the higher-earning spouse who claims benefits early, the lower-earning spouse who claims their own worker benefit early, or the spouse who claims spousal benefits early.

When you claim early on your own work record, the reduction formula is divided into two parts: a reduction factor representing the months between age 62 and age 65 (the original FRA for everyone) and a different reduction factor representing the months after 65 to your FRA. The reduction calculation is:

- 5/9 of 1% for each month during the first 36 months (20% reduction); and
- 5/12 of 1% for each month that falls in the next 24 months (10% further reduction).

This explains how Social Security imposes up to a 30% penalty for those with an FRA of 67 who claim benefits between age 62 and FRA.

Reductions for spouses' early benefits versus for workers

The rules and penalties for dependent spouses differ from those for workers. If you're the spouse eligible for a spousal benefit or top-up and claim it before reaching your own FRA, your spousal portion will be reduced according to a different formula. For each month you claim early, your payment is cut by a specific percentage that is higher than it would be on a worker's record:

- 25/36 of 1% for each month during the first 36 months (25% reduction); plus,
- 5/12 of 1% for each month that falls in the next 24 months (10% reduction).

If a spouse with an FRA of 67 claims at 62, they'll receive a full 35% reduction on the spousal benefit. If the wife earns less, her starting point is half of his PIA. For example, if his PIA is $2,000 per month, her spousal benefit at FRA is $1,000 per month. However, if she claims at 62, her benefit drops to $650 per month – a whopping 35% reduction.

That's not to say she shouldn't claim at 62 if that supports the couple's retirement income plan. There are many reasons why the lower earner (usually the wife, but not always) might want to claim early.

- She may be much younger than her spouse, and they want to spend their early retirement years together.
- She may need to or want to care for her grandchildren.
- She might need to care for a sick parent, spouse, or friend.
- They have saved money to retire early, and receiving Social Security helps the couple achieve their dream.

The bottom line is to make an early claiming decision with your eyes wide open. Understand that this decision is usually permanent and generally cannot be undone. Giving up 30% or 35% of your Social Security income each month over a 30-year retirement is a big deal. Make sure you know your options and understand the consequences of your decisions. Too often, people say they didn't know. Well, now you know!

A note about the Restricted Application

People born in the early 1950s who are married believe they have access to more benefits than just their own. That was true at one time. Unfortunately, people born after 1954 also think they have an additional way to access more Social Security benefits than they are permitted.

Here's the situation: If you were born before January 2, 1954, were married, and filed taxes jointly, there was a loophole in the Social Security law. It inadvertently allowed one spouse to claim just their spousal benefit when they reached FRA. This way, their spousal benefits started at age 66, while their own PIA, based on their work record, increased by 8% per year with Delayed Retirement Credits. Then, at age 70, they would switch to a much higher benefit based on their own work record.

Practically speaking, this meant that many married women who had their own work record could claim half of their spouses' PIAs when they reached their FRA of 66. Then they would wait until age 70 to request their own significantly higher payments. This gave them four additional years of Social Security benefits AND a much higher payout when they turned 70.

That strategy was called "claim now, claim more later." That is clearly not in line with Social Security's goals for fairness. Therefore, this unintended consequence was addressed as part of the Bipartisan Budget Act of 2015. I mention it here only because a high percentage of married people still believe they can receive extra benefits. They are none too happy when they learn this mistake in the law was corrected over 10 years ago!

Note: The Restricted Application also applied to husbands if they met the age requirement. A husband could claim only his spousal benefit when reaching FRA of 66 if his spouse was already claiming, allowing him to delay his own benefit until age 70 to maximize monthly benefits.

Every couple's situation is different

There are no hard and fast rules about the best time to claim your own Social Security benefits. There are, however, many strong opinions! Some financial professionals firmly believe you should wait until age 70, while others think you should claim at 62. There are many options in between those two age goal posts.

What I will say here is that it is incredibly important not to make your claiming decision in isolation. Do not believe all the hysterical headlines. Do not take a financial advisor's advice on Social Security without a comprehensive retirement income plan that shows you the options and trade-offs. And definitely do not just claim because Congress is sitting on the sidelines doing nothing to shore up this incredibly important social safety net that happens to be burnt around the edges.

In the upcoming chapters, you'll meet several couples, each with different backgrounds, situations, and earnings histories. See if your circumstances are similar to any of theirs. Read their stories and discover what options they might consider when deciding how and when to claim their Social Security benefits.

- Sandy and Steve followed traditional household roles. What will their best Social Security claiming strategy be?

- Mike and Melissa are an unusual couple from the Baby Boomer generation. She's the doctor, and he'd be a starving artist without her.

- Dwight and Amanda met when he began working at the same company where she had been employed for years.

She's already claiming Social Security. Will she be eligible for a spousal top-up?

You'll find an action plan and checklist for married couples on Boomer Retirement Briefs at https://boomerretirementbriefs.com.

Please keep in mind that while there can be many routes to take, making final decisions depends on two key elements: a comprehensive retirement income plan and a pretty good idea of what to do with your time in retirement.

CHAPTER 12:

The "Traditional" Husband and Wife Couple

Sandy and Steve are what many call a traditional married couple with conventional household roles. They married in their mid-20s and started a family right away. Over the next nine years, they had four children. Steve's first job was in sales, which required a lot of travel. They moved several times as he received promotions and climbed the corporate ladder. It was an easy decision for them that Sandy would stay home to manage their home and the children while Steve pursued career advancement. Sandy always wanted to stay home when she had kids to be involved in their schools and use her creative and artistic skills to support their upbringing.

As the kids got older and more independent, Sandy found time to engage in more volunteer work in her community. She initiated a reading program at the library and assisted a friend in starting a cycling team that raises money for children's cancer research. She enjoyed hosting social events at her house, ranging from book clubs and ladies' painting parties to backyard barbecues and large family holiday celebrations.

Both she and Steve knew that her role was important and that they were better off as a family with this arrangement.

Retirement is sneaking up on them. Will their ideas work?

Because Steve's promotions came fairly frequently, they could make saving for retirement a priority. Steve took advantage of his 401(k) at work, and Sandy set up and contributed to her own IRAs (individual retirement accounts) over the years.

Their plan is for Steve to work until at least age 65, when he'll be eligible for Medicare. There is a three-year age difference between them, so they'll need to figure out options for Sandy's health insurance if he retires before she turns 65 and becomes eligible for Medicare. They are wondering whether Steve should plan to work until 68 instead of retiring at 65. Will that be the best overall strategy when considering both Social Security benefits and health insurance coverage?

An initial look at Social Security

Several factors need consideration for each spouse, including how much Sandy's spousal benefit will be. Since Sandy worked only four years before staying home to raise her family, she does not qualify for Social Security retirement benefits based on her own work record. However, she is eligible for spousal benefits. When she reaches her Full Retirement Age (FRA) of 66 and 10 months, she can start receiving 50% of Steve's Primary Insurance Amount (PIA). He will need to be claiming his benefit already, but since he's three years older, that may work out well.

Another factor is that Steve's retirement date can be different from when he claims his Social Security benefit. He might retire at, say, 63. As long as they have other means to pay their living expenses, he wouldn't need to claim Social Security until a later date—at FRA, at 68, or as late as age 70. Just because someone retires from a job, or is asked to retire, doesn't mean they have to tap Social Security at the same time.

It's not just about the numbers

A closer look at Sandy and Steve's numbers will lay the ground-work for decision-making. Steve reaches FRA at 66 years, 4 months. Sandy's FRA is when she turns 66 and 10 months. Here's a look at some of their combined claiming options (all numbers are approximate):

Steve's age when claiming:	Monthly benefit:	Sandy's age when claiming:	Monthly benefit:	Total Social Security income
At his FRA: 66 and 4 months	$3,400	At age 63	$1,200	$4,600
At age 65	$3,100	At age 62	$1,120	$4,220
At age 68	$3,850	At age 65	$1,440	$5,290
At age 70	$4,400	At her FRA: 66 and 10 months	$1,700	$6,100

Like most married couples, there isn't a single best answer for when to claim benefits. Sandy and Steve should consider several important factors before making their decision, including:

- When does Steve want to retire? What is realistic given his job? Will the company keep him on the job until he turns 68?

- What other resources can they access if they plan to wait until Steve's FRA or later to claim Social Security benefits?

- What options will they have for Sandy's health insurance before she turns 65 and becomes eligible for Medicare? How much will it cost, and do they have the money?

Although waiting until 70 gives Steve the highest monthly benefit, it does not change Sandy's monthly benefit. The maximum Sandy can receive is 50% of Steve's PIA, which is $1,700 per month.

If Steve claims at 65, Sandy will be 62 and eligible to claim as well. However, she'll receive the smallest amount of her spousal benefit – about $1,120 per month. She doesn't have to claim that early, but she could.

Steve can still claim a reduced benefit at 65, and Sandy could wait until she turns 65, which would increase her monthly benefit to $1,440.

The decision Steve makes will also impact Sandy if she becomes a widow. As a widow, Sandy would lose her spousal benefit but would receive the amount Steve was collecting. Thinking about the survivor's benefit is a key factor for all couples. In fact, it's often the most important consideration in deciding when to claim. (More about survivor benefits in later chapters.)

Making the decision is not so easy

This situation highlights several financial realities for couples in traditional household roles. One key point is that at-home wives can receive at most half of their husbands' PIA as Social Security income. While this certainly benefits the household's financial situation, it's important to remember that it may take several years before the wife can collect her full benefits.

Also, keep in mind that it can be challenging to choose the best option when benefit amounts vary significantly. It seems clear that Steve should wait until age 70 to claim, even though Sandy won't receive any Social Security income until she reaches FRA. As a dependent spouse, she cannot claim early (and reduced) spousal benefits until Steve has filed for his.

Their original question was whether Steve could retire at 65 and start both Social Security and Medicare. If he does, and Sandy claims at the same time (she'll be 62), they would receive $1,880 less in monthly income than if they wait until he's 70 and she's 67. Sandy could still wait to claim her spousal benefit at 65, but that only increases her benefit by about $320 per month.

A complete retirement income plan is essential

Their claiming decisions cannot be based solely on a table of Social Security options. This couple needs a comprehensive retirement income plan. They will have to consider their Social Security decisions in the context of all their other resources and financial goals.

- They might have millions saved for retirement, so they'll wait until they turn 70 and 67 to maximize their Social Security benefits.

- Perhaps Steve decides to work until 70 to delay claiming, and his employer is willing to keep him on the payroll.

- With four children to put through college, they may not have saved enough for retirement. They may find it a financial necessity for Steve to start Social Security right away if he retires early.

- They need to understand the tax consequences of each claiming option versus tapping into tax-deferred assets first.

Based on Steve's questions and his clear desire to retire before age 70, it might be better for him to claim benefits at 65 or at his FRA. This allows him to draw less from their portfolio, hopefully preserving more for a family legacy.

Realistically, even if Steve decides it is best to keep working, his company might have other plans, and his job could end sooner than he expects. The key is to begin exploring different possibilities based on an overall retirement income strategy and to start mapping out different scenarios at ages 50, 55, and 60.

Summary

Is it better for Sandy and Steve to prioritize time or maximize their Social Security income? Each couple must decide how to balance their opportunities. There is no wrong choice as long as each person understands the trade-offs.

Married women and men who do not qualify for Social Security retirement benefits based on their own work records should keep a few key points in mind:

- They are entitled to their own retirement benefits based on the wage earner spouse's work record.

- They will receive 50% of the worker's PIA only when they claim at their own FRA. They'll get less if claiming earlier, and will not receive a higher amount by waiting until after their FRA.

- They cannot claim spousal benefits until the spouse with the work record has claimed their own benefit. The two must come as a dancing duo into Social Security retirement benefits.

CHAPTER 13:

She's the Doctor,
He's the Starving Artist

Mike and Melissa are somewhat unusual among the older Baby
Boomers. They married young in the 1970s, and she has been
the sole breadwinner for 40 years. She's a physician and the department chair at a large Midwest hospital system. He was an
at-home dad and has been "dabbling" in art for decades. They
are funny, smart, and still in love after 45 years together. They
are both tradition-busters and have been ahead of their time
throughout their years together. Melissa was born in December
1952. She was still working when I met them and planned to
continue for at least a few more years, likely until age 70. She
signed up for Medicare when she turned 65. Mike was born in
1954, so he is a couple of years younger.

Mike asked the original question that sparked our discussion:
"My wife is the higher earner, and I don't qualify for Social
Security. Is it possible for a 'trophy husband' to get anything
from Social Security? If so, can I start now?"

Non-wage-earning spouses, even husbands,
get benefits

Well, yes and no. In short, Mike will indeed get his own retirement benefit as a "trophy husband," but he cannot claim his
spousal benefit until Melissa claims her benefit. He will qualify

for half of Melissa's Primary Insurance Amount (PIA) once he reaches his Full Retirement Age (FRA) at 66.

They were very surprised to learn that Mike could receive any Social Security benefits at all, since he didn't work long enough to earn 40 credits. Melissa mentioned that she knew she had to sign up for Medicare as soon as she was nearing age 65, but she had never heard that spouses who don't earn wages, and husbands in particular, could be eligible for spousal benefits.

She is in good company. The vast majority of non-wage-earning spouses have no idea they are entitled to their own Social Security retirement benefits, whether they are wives or husbands.

Mike was very happy to learn that he is entitled to up to half of Melissa's benefit amount. He felt somewhat valued and validated that his role as the "trophy husband and all-around great dad" (his description, not hers, but she did agree after a short pause) would be recognized at retirement. They are both delighted that their household income will be higher than they expected once they are both claiming Social Security. In fact, they will see about 33% more income from Social Security while both are alive. That was quite a bonus to learn about, and now they are rethinking when Melissa might retire.

When should she claim?

Melissa reached her FRA of 66 in 2018. Mike reached his in 2020. Since she hadn't started collecting Social Security yet, they could time Melissa's claiming strategy to align with Mike's FRA, when she will be 68 and he 66. Or she could wait until age 70 to claim her maximum benefit, at which point Mike would be 68. Although Mike would miss out on two years of benefits, the survivor benefit during their later years would be maximized.

Another option is for Melissa to start claiming her benefit now and keep working. Since she's past her FRA, she can get her full PIA plus some delayed retirement credits she has already earned, along with her full-time paycheck from the hospital. This lets Mike claim his spousal benefit now; however, since he's younger than his FRA, his benefit would be reduced.

Here's a look at how their benefits might turn out (all numbers are approximate):

Melissa's Age	Melissa's Social Security benefit	Mike's Age	Mike's Spousal Benefit	Total Household Income From Social Security	Surviving Spouse's Benefit
66 (FRA)	$2,800	64	$1,180	$4,000	$2,800
67	$3,020	65	$1,280	$4,300	$3,020
68	$3,260	66 (FRA)	$1,400	$4,660	$3,260
69	$3,520	67	$1,400	$4,920	$3,520
70	$3,800	68	$1,400	$5,200	$3,800

Mike only receives his full 50% of Melissa's PIA when he claims at his FRA. Melissa will be 68 at that time. She could choose to retire then and start her claim two years earlier than planned. She won't receive the maximum from Social Security, but she still earns two years of delayed retirement credits, roughly 16% more. Plus, Mike gets to claim his maximum spousal benefit two years earlier.

The other factor to consider is how Melissa's claim impacts the surviving spouse. While both are alive, they receive two Social Security checks, but once the first spouse dies the lower benefit stops. The higher Melissa's payment is, the more income remains in the household for the surviving spouse. This is a case where getting more is better. Sometimes, more is just more. And that's a positive thing.

It's just a little disappointing

Mike was so excited about this newfound income that he wanted to claim right away. But that's not an option for him unless Melissa decides to claim now.

While it was fun to think about retiring and claiming benefits right then, they knew they needed time to work out all their numbers and develop a complete retirement income plan. It was just a little disappointing for Mike that they had to work as a joint unit and claim based on Melissa's record and her entry into Social Security. For married couples where one spouse doesn't earn wages, they essentially share a single work record. But the one with the earnings history opens the gate.

Looking ahead

The good news is that Mike has newfound income in retirement. The catch is that the wage earner with the record must jump into the Social Security pool first.

There's more good news: they don't have much longer to wait before Melissa retires. Melissa enjoys her job. She can use these last few years to figure out what she'll do after the demands of her job end. No more 3:00 a.m. baby deliveries. No more emergency calls from new moms. No more 36-hour labors.

Deciding when and how to claim Social Security benefits is often just as much about personal readiness and timing—and about spending more time together in the early golden years—as it is about the money.

Summary

Melissa and Mike are a married couple living in a "traditional" arrangement where one person is the breadwinner and the other stays home. However, in their case, the "traditional" roles are reversed. Among the younger generations, at-home dads are becoming more common. But it was not at all common in the 20th century. By the end of this century, it would be great to see parents share roles in a much more equal way.

To Social Security, it doesn't matter which spouse is the higher earner or who stays at home. Of course, this setup was almost unthinkable back in the 1930s. A man staying home to raise the kids and manage the household? Not a chance. But in the end, for Social Security, it's all about the numbers. Go dads!

CHAPTER 14:

She's Older and Ready to Claim. Will She Get a Spousal "Top-Up?"

Dwight and Amanda met when he started working at the same hospital where she had worked for years. They were both divorced after short marriages (he was married for six years in his 20s; she was married for three years). They were quite "smitten" from the start and dated for four years. They wanted to ensure this marriage would succeed. Their concern was their age gap: she is nine years older than he is.

Married for 20 years, they are doing well. He's 53, and she's 62. Amanda, a nurse in various surgical units and the emergency department for nearly 40 years, is exhausted. She wants to retire early, but they're unsure if that would be the best financial decision.

A pension and Social Security offer a way out

The hospital offers a pension plan. Amanda is eligible for $1,500 per month starting at age 62. She could receive more if she waits until 65, but early retirement is her priority. In addition, the hospital is a covered employer, so she is on track to receive Social Security retirement benefits of about $1,800 per month at her Full Retirement Age (FRA) of 67. If she retires at 62 and claims Social Security early, she would receive a reduced benefit of roughly $1,260 per month.

Overall, she will bring in $2,760 per month as an early retiree. This amount is less than her current income, but with some adjustments, like cutting back on certain expenses and cooking at home more often, both of them support her early retirement plans. However, they want to verify one detail about her Social Security: when Dwight retires and starts claiming his own benefit, will hers increase? And if so, by how much?

Dwight's Social Security situation is key

To answer that, we need to know Dwight's Social Security estimates. He works on the technology side of hospital operations and earns a good, above-average salary. His last statement indicated that he was on track for a $4,000 retirement benefit if he claims Social Security at his FRA. He's still a long way from getting a final estimate, and this projection assumes he continues to work at the same income level until reaching FRA.

His early estimate also shows that if he claims at 62, the benefit amount would be reduced by 30% to $2,800. If he waits until 70 before claiming, he'll receive a 24% increase in monthly income to nearly $5,000. These are all preliminary estimates, but they give the couple a look at the possibilities based on current laws today—and assuming Congress takes some action to strengthen the program.

Dwight is also eligible for a pension of about $2,500 per month if he waits until age 65 to retire.

The main focus for this couple is their time together. Retirement involves balancing time and money. Some couples prefer more leisure time together, even if that requires financial compromises. Often, couples with a significant age difference want to make the most of their time together.

If Dwight waits to retire until his mid-60s, Amanda would be in her mid-70s. If he waits to claim Social Security until age

70, Amanda will be 79. While they expect to live a long time in retirement, arthritis is already making it harder for Amanda to do some of the activities she loves, especially gardening, and Dwight admits to being in better shape some 25 years ago. Therefore, making the most of their early retirement years is a top priority.

What happens to each of their retirement benefits depends on when Dwight retires and decides to claim.

- If he retires at his FRA, he will be 67 and Amanda 76. His Social Security income would be $4,000.

- If he retires and claims at 62, his reduced benefit would be approximately $2,800 per month.

- If he retires and claims at 65, when his pension benefit reaches the maximum payout, his monthly Social Security payment would be about $3,500.

Figuring out Amanda's spousal benefit

How do spousal benefits work when Amanda has also earned a benefit on her own work history? There are several steps to determine a spouse's benefit when there are two options on the table.

- Amanda's maximum spousal benefit is 50% of Dwight's PIA, but only if she claims at her FRA. Half of Dwight's PIA is $2,000 per month.

- She is therefore eligible for a calculated spousal "top-up" of $200. (Her maximum spousal benefit of $2,000 minus her own PIA of $1,800.)

- She cannot claim this spousal benefit until Dwight claims his benefit. Since she will be well past her own FRA when Dwight becomes eligible to claim, she will receive the top-up of $200 per month at that time.

Eventually, she will receive two payments: her own benefit and a spousal top-up. For the first nine years of her retirement, she will receive her own reduced worker benefit of $1,260 per month, with annual increases for COLA. After Dwight claims, her spousal top-up will become available. It will be higher than $200 due to Dwight's actual earnings and annual COLAs.

Whenever Dwight claims, whether at 62, 65, or 67, Amanda's top-up amount remains the same. It is a calculated value based on Dwight's PIA, regardless of when he actually claims. However, he must claim before her top-up becomes available.

Assuming she'll receive about $200 extra as a spousal top-up, it will help offset the 30% reduction in Dwight's monthly benefit if he claims at 62. He would get a payment roughly $1,200 less than if he waits until his FRA. However, waiting those five years to claim means Amanda must wait until she is 76 before she receives any spousal top-up. By then, their years together may be fewer than they want.

Other options may be available

Amanda might choose to retire at 62, but then consider finding some part-time work. This could be in her nursing field, a related area, or at a garden shop. Any income she earns could impact the amount of Social Security benefits she receives (see discussion about the Earnings Limit in Part 3), but it might also help with some of the financial challenges of living in retirement. Additionally, it could ultimately raise her own monthly benefit.

Another option could be for Dwight to phase into retirement. There might be an opportunity at his current employer to work three days a week or in some other part-time arrangement. As a technology expert, he may also find additional consulting or short-term opportunities. That might allow him to step off the full-time track earlier but delay claiming Social Security.

Summary

Couples with significant age gaps often view their situation in two particular ways.

1. If time is the priority, the younger spouse might claim at 62, locking in a reduced benefit for their retirement.
2. If money is the priority, they should forgo early retirement and wait to claim until at least FRA.

Time, health, and the desire to enjoy the best years of retirement are major factors in most people's claiming decisions. The key to making good decisions is to review your entire retirement income plan and determine if and where you are willing to make other trade-offs.

Be creative in your thinking. There are many more opportunities for work in your 60s now than in previous times. New work-from-home opportunities didn't exist until the COVID-19 pandemic. And more small businesses are looking for part-time or seasonal help. See what will work for you and your spouse. There is no right or wrong answer, just something new to do with some of your time.

SECTION 2C
Information for Divorced Individuals

CHAPTER 15:

The Basics of Claiming on Your Ex-Spouse

One of the biggest Social Security surprises happens when divorced women discover they can claim benefits based on their ex-husbands' work records. It's even more surprising when an ex-husband finds out he might be eligible to claim benefits from an ex-wife. The usual responses I get are, "Are you kidding me?" and "Are you sure?"

Here's one case where something sounds a little too good to be true. Approaching it with a healthy dose of skepticism is a good idea. But, no, I am not kidding, and yes, I am sure.

Many divorced women and low-wage-earning men discover that their retirement might not be quite as bleak as they thought. That's because they may qualify for ex-spousal benefits based on their exes' work histories. In most cases, the ex-husband was the higher earner, so the ex-wife might receive a higher monthly benefit. However, Social Security treats all genders equally, so if the husband was the lower earner, he may well qualify for ex-spousal benefits.

Social Security recognizes that together spouses form an economic unit, and as such, each spouse will be provided with a social safety net in retirement – even if that union didn't last. For much of 20th-century history, a woman's primary role was to stay home and care for the children. Even if she worked for wages, it was secondary to her husband's career and earning power. Although this is not necessarily the case today, with many women holding powerful jobs with significant salaries, it still applies to many women entering retirement today.

Women's financial independence influences divorce rates

Even in the 1930s, as the Social Security Act was being draft-ed, divorce was increasing. This was partly due to popu-lation growth—more marriages led to more divorces—and partly because women's economic independence was ex-panding. Ultimately, more women had the means to leave unhappy marriages.

- In 1930, there were some 196,000 divorces.

- In 1960, nearly 400,000 divorces occurred.

- By 1980, about 1.2 million divorces were granted.

- Another 1.2 million in 1990.

The number of divorces has been declining since the turn of the 21st century, but the total number of divorced people re-mains high.[11]

The designers of Social Security initially did not address di-vorced spouses. They were not insured with even a modest social safety net of income in retirement. As the number of divorced women without their own work records increased over the years, their need for a retirement safety net became more urgent. In 1965, changes in Social Security provided re-tirement benefits for divorced women who had been in long-term marriages.

Tens of millions of divorced women are living in retirement. Earning enough income to support themselves for 20 or 30 years is often a difficult journey. The fact that many divorced women can receive a Social Security benefit that is higher than what they could collect based on their own work record makes a real and lasting difference for many. It also helps meet Social Security's goal of lifting more older Americans out of poverty.

Motherhood and divorce

Becoming a mother is one of the most significant roles a woman can ever play. Frequently, mothers scale back successful careers to spend both quality and quantity time raising their children. The percentage of women who step off the career path for at least a few years to stay at home has remained relatively steady since the late 1980s. In fact, 28% of moms stayed home full-time in 1990, 29% in 2010, and 32% in 2018. The lowest point for mothers staying at home was in the early 2000s, when about 23% of moms were at home.[12]

So, what happens if you leave the career track and later get divorced? Neither person gains financially from a divorce, but mothers are disproportionately affected. They have significantly reduced their work histories, and many will reenter the workforce with lower earning potential. Nearly all (98%) divorced individuals who receive alimony are women, but the amount they get usually falls far short of what they would have earned if they had continued working. The cycle of moving in and out of employment often causes financial harm both during working years and in retirement.

As mentioned earlier, women's Social Security payments are notably lower than men's. This is especially true for divorced women, particularly if they are single parents. Therefore, it can be a great relief at retirement to discover that monthly benefits might be higher as an ex-spouse than based on an individual's own inconsistent earnings record.

What about divorced men and custodial dads?

For the current population of near-retirees, we're referring to the youngest Baby Boomers who turned 65 in 2025 and the oldest Gen Xers who reached 60. Many of these men were part of marriages that ended in divorce. We know from re-marriage records that 66% of divorced Boomer men married again at least once. In contrast, only about 40% of divorced Boomer women remarried. The percentage of men and women remarrying before age 65 is closer, with 71% of men and 63% of women.[13]

When a divorce involves children, they tend to live with the mother by a large margin. Not always, of course, but in these older age groups or near retirees, that was more common. Some stats and facts on divorced dads:[14]

- In 2018, there were 12.9 million custodial parents nationwide; 80% were mothers and 20% were fathers.

- 27% of children living primarily with their mothers lived in poverty versus 11% when living with custodial fathers.

- 74% of custodial fathers were more likely to be employed full time compared to just half of divorced moms with children living with them.

- Custodial mothers are more likely to participate in at least one public assistance program (45% versus 26% for custodial fathers).

But is there a catch?

Well, a little. Not every divorced person will qualify for a payment based on their ex. There are several requirements to meet. The first is the length of the marriage. An "economic union" must have been established to be eligible to claim on an ex. Social Security defines this as being married for 10 consecutive years or longer. And there is no rounding up.

If you were married for 9 years and 10 months, that is not 10 years. You will not qualify for benefits on your ex. If you were married for 6 years, then divorced, and later remarried the same person for another 8 years? Not 10 consecutive years. The only small exception is if you were married, divorced, and remarried within 12 months to the same person. Social Security considers this as consecutive years. You still need to be married for at least 10 years overall, but the four- or five-month break won't count against you.

Eligible ex-spouse benefits depend on a series of rules

If you meet the 10-year marriage rule, you might qualify for a benefit on your ex's record. However, there are other criteria you must also satisfy:

- Each of you must reach age 62 before either can claim an ex-spouse benefit. That's because no one can claim retirement benefits before age 62, so both must reach this age for either to qualify.

  - If you are the younger spouse, you can claim benefits as early as age 62, since your ex will already be 62 or older.

  - If you are the older spouse, you must wait until your ex's 62nd birthday before you can claim ex-spousal benefits. This usually isn't an issue if the exes are close in age, but suppose you are seven years older. You turn 62, but your ex is only 55. You cannot file for or receive ex-spousal benefits because the younger ex isn't 62 yet. You can still apply on your own work record, but you'll wait a considerable amount of time before you can claim ex-spousal benefits based on your ex.

- Your ex does not have to be claiming Social Security. Unlike married couples, divorced individuals do not have to wait for their ex to claim. Each person jumps into separate pools at different times.

- Your divorce must have been finalized at least two years ago. In other words, you can't get a divorce and start collecting benefits as an ex-spouse immediately. There is a waiting period. The exception is if your ex is already collecting benefits. In that case, you can start collecting right away, as long as you're at least 62.

- Last, but not least, you must be unmarried to collect as an ex-spouse. That may seem obvious, but it is a point of confusion for many divorced folks.

Let's say a woman was married to her first husband for 15 years, then divorced. Several years later, she remarried and has been married to her second husband for eight years. When it comes time to claim, it might seem that she has a choice: either claim based on her ex or claim based on her current spouse – whichever offers the larger benefit. But that's not how the rules work. You don't get to cherry-pick which person you claim on in this situation. Since you are married (and hopefully, happily married!) to husband number two, your only claiming options are your own work record or as a current spouse eligible for spousal benefits.

What if you end up divorcing spouse number two after 10 or more years of marriage? Well, that's a different story. In that case, you can claim on whichever ex's record gives you the higher amount. Keep in mind, all the other rules also have to be met, including that both exes must be 62 or older, both divorces were at least two years ago, etc.

Ex-husbands who remarry are concerned about lower benefits

There's good news here for all ex-spouses who remarried. Your own calculated benefit won't be affected if your ex claims ex-spousal benefits on your work record. One of the biggest myths about Social Security is that the higher-earning ex-spouse will be cheated out of (usually) his benefits because his ex is tapping into them.

Not so. That isn't how the math works. Back in chapter 6, you can review how your PIA is calculated. It's based on your work history and wages. The first step is determining your AIME. The second step is calculating your PIA. The actuaries have already baked in the PIA calculation that others may be paid from your record.

In other words, the fact that some folks will be divorced, some will be widows, and some will be dependent children is already included in each PIA calculation. You will not lose any benefits unless you personally choose to claim before your FRA. That decision is yours to make. The benefit estimate shown on your statement is the one you can rely on.

How the ex-spousal claim works

Let me put a few fears to rest. If you're divorced, your ex will never know if you claim on their work record and receive an ex-spousal benefit. You don't ask for their permission. You don't talk to them or consult with them. This is strictly an arrangement between you and the Social Security Administration.

Also, as mentioned earlier, if you are the ex whose Primary Insurance Amount (PIA) is too high to qualify for an ex-spousal benefit, you won't be cheated out of your own benefit. And you won't know if your ex received an ex-spousal top-up benefit or not.

If you are the former spouse and think you might increase your payments by claiming on your ex's work record, you will need to schedule a confidential one-on-one, in-person meeting with your local Social Security office or arrange a phone appointment. You will be asked to provide key documents to prove your identity and the marriage, plus show the divorce decree.

The Social Security agent will run calculations for you. They'll review benefit amounts based on your work record and your ex's record. Since you can't access your ex's work history, Social Security will handle the calculations and explain how you can receive a benefit based on the options available. The higher amount is the one you will get. Let's look at a couple of examples to see how ex-spousal benefits work.

Example 1: Amber and Andy

Amber and Andy were married for 18 years. Today, they are both 62, and their divorce was 20 years ago. Amber has not remarried and wants to know if she can receive a higher retirement benefit based on Andy's work history. He earned more during their marriage, as she left paid work for 15 years to raise their children. She believes he continued working after that, but she isn't sure if she can get a higher benefit.

From her Social Security statement, Amber sees that her benefit is estimated at $1,600 per month once she reaches her Full Retirement Age (FRA). If she claims early, her benefit will be reduced—by 30% if she claims at 62—to about $1,120 per month. It would be quite challenging to cover her basic expenses in retirement on such a limited income.

She schedules a private meeting with the Social Security office, and they pull up Andy's work record. He continued to work and earned a healthy salary over the years. His Primary Insurance Amount (PIA) is estimated at $3,800 per month. Amber's benefit, boosted by an ex-spousal top-up, will be $1,900 per month if she waits until her FRA. Her top-up of $300 per month will be helpful during retirement.

If she claims at any time before her FRA, this ex-spousal benefit amount will be reduced. If she claims at 62, both benefits will be reduced as follows:

- Her own worker benefit will be reduced by about 30%, and

- Her ex-spousal top-up benefit would be cut by about 35%.

She'd still receive a higher amount than the reduced benefit solely based on her work history.

This is good news for Amber. Andy won't realize that her claim is partially based on his work record. Also, nothing happens to Andy's monthly benefit. If he waits until his FRA to claim, he'll still get his $3,800 per month. There is no reduction or "loss of benefits" because his ex is claiming on his record.

If Andy has remarried, Amber's ex-spousal claim does not affect his current wife. If she is eligible for spousal benefits, she would also receive $1,900 at her FRA.

Example 2: Betty and Brian

Betty and Brian married in 1980, and their marriage lasted just over 10 years. Betty never remarried, but Brian did. Assuming all other requirements are met, Betty's ex-spousal benefit can be considered based on Brian's work history. Even though the divorce was three decades ago.

After the divorce, Betty decided to continue her professional career, and her PIA is $3,200 per month. Brian's PIA is $3,250 per month.

In this case, Betty will not receive any ex-spousal top-up based on Brian's work history. Her own work and wage history were strong. As an ex-spouse, Betty's ex-spousal benefit would be calculated at half of Brian's PIA, or $1,625 per month. However, her own record of $3,200 per month is significantly higher, so after consulting with the Social Security agent, she'll see that she has earned her own higher benefit. That is the only benefit she is eligible for—and the highest one she can receive.

The same goes for Brian. He can also check with Social Security to see if his retirement benefit might increase. There's no top-up available as an ex-spouse because he remarried. But could there be a top-up from his current wife's work history? Since his benefit is significantly high, he won't be eligible, even if his current wife has a PIA of $4,000. His own benefit is much higher than half of his current wife's in this example.

Do ex-spousal benefits seem fair?

To some, it seems odd that divorced individuals might receive a higher retirement benefit based on an ex-spouse they were married to 30 years ago. The couple was young and just starting out, so neither might have been earning significant wages. Years later, the ex who never remarried might qualify for a larger benefit because they were once married to someone who later built a successful career.

Although a marriage didn't make it through decades, there was still a significant investment at one point. Divorced individuals deserve dignity in retirement. Both exes, and usually the ex-wife, deserve not to live in poverty. That's the goal and foundation of the entire Social Security law that was established when the country was desperately trying to recover after the Great Depression.

Keep in mind, these benefits are not designed to make anyone rich. Social Security is a form of social insurance that helps prevent our oldest citizens from falling into poverty—even an ex-spouse. The contributions made to the program already account for supporting both spouses during retirement.

It's interesting to note that divorce benefits are not one-sided. They are not only benefits for an ex-wife. If the ex-wife is the higher earner, her ex-spouse can and should claim benefits based on her work record. The same rules apply to men and women alike. While the original rule was created to protect women who are divorced from men, it now allows the lower-earning spouse to receive retirement benefits regardless of gender.

Divorce decrees cannot reduce ex-spousal Social Security benefits

It is distressing to hear from divorced women who say they "signed away their rights" to their spousal benefits during the divorce process. Unfortunately, some attorneys think this is allowed and include a clause in the divorce agreement stating that the ex-wife cannot claim Social Security benefits on her ex-spouse's record.

This is simply not allowed. If this language is in your divorce decree, it is neither valid nor enforceable. Meet with Social Security to get your money!

Divorce rules apply to same sex married couples

Now that same sex married couples qualify for retirement spousal benefits, ex-spousal benefits also apply. If your marriage did not last, you may still be eligible for retirement benefits based on your ex-wife or ex-husband. In 2025, we marked the 10-year anniversary of the Supreme Court ruling in Obergefell v. Hodges, which legalized and recognized same-sex marriage. Some states adopted these laws even earlier.

This is important because the same eligibility rules for divorced spouses apply: you must have been married for 10 consecutive years or longer, both of you need to be 62 or older, you must not be remarried, and the divorce must have been final at least two years ago or your ex is already claiming benefits. Plus, you would be the ex-spouse who receives a higher benefit by claiming on your ex.

You'll need to bring the necessary documentation to your local Social Security office, where an agent will assist you in determining how to receive the maximum benefit you qualify for.

Divorced individuals have many questions

In the chapters that follow in this section, you'll meet two remarkable women who are divorced and working hard to create income in retirement. You'll also hear about their ex-husbands, who asked several questions that you might have wondered about as well. For more information on avoiding divorce pitfalls and a checklist and action plan for claiming Social Security when you're divorced, visit Boomer Retirement Briefs at https://boomerretirementbriefs.com/.

Read on for the following stories:

- Patricia is a registered nurse who is divorced and a single mom. She'd like to tap into her Social Security benefit early.

- Deborah is lively and charming. She was married for years, then divorced, and tickled to be able to claim on her ex.

CHAPTER 16:

Divorced and Working: Should I Claim at FRA to Help Pay the Bills?

Patricia is a registered nurse. She and Peter were married for 30 years before they divorced. Their adopted daughter is a junior in college. Patricia is turning 65 this year, enjoys her job, and has no specific plans for retirement. She was thinking it would be nice to travel more and pay for her daughter's last three semesters of college. She wonders about claiming Social Security now to increase her income.

Patricia asked, "Is it true that I can take my Social Security benefit while working without a decrease in my benefit? That way, I could get some extra money now."

This is a good question to ask. Several layers of her personal situation must be considered before answering her question. Let's take a closer look.

Answering Patricia's initial question

Let me first answer her direct question: Is it true that you can claim Social Security while working? Yes, indeed you can. However, if you are younger than FRA and working, you might not receive a Social Security payment every month. There is an earnings limit test to pass first. If she earns more than a certain dollar amount in the years before reaching FRA, some of her benefits could be withheld until the month she reaches FRA. (Read more about the earnings limit in Part 3.)

Social Security has a specific definition for "retirement." The most obvious one is the month you stop working and stop receiving a paycheck. But there is another definition unique to Social Security: you are deemed retired once you reach your Full Retirement Age. Whether you are still working after reaching FRA or not does not matter. If you continue working, you are still deemed retired. That means you can earn any amount of income and still collect your full Social Security benefits once you reach your FRA.

Patricia was born in 1960, so her FRA is the month she turns 67. Once she reaches 67, she can work as much or as little as she wants, claim Social Security, and receive her full retirement benefit without any reductions or withholdings.

In her situation, it might be a good idea to bring in some extra cash each month, even though she has not yet reached FRA. She's eligible for about $2,000 per month at FRA. That's her Primary Insurance Amount (PIA), and that amount is paid only at her FRA.

But what if she claims six months earlier instead? Well, she would lock in a reduced benefit of about $1,930 per month, or approximately a 3.33% decrease in benefits. Depending on the specific timing and her income before FRA, she may have a clawback due to the earnings limit. But the extra money would be a helpful boost to enjoy some of the things that are important to her. And help her daughter with college payments.

But wait, there's more

However, she still does not have a complete picture of her situation. Patricia needs to resolve four other important considerations before filing a claim:

- First, as an ex-spouse, she might qualify for a higher benefit based on her ex-husband's record. Let's say Peter's PIA is $3,900 a month. Patricia's benefit as an ex-spouse would then be about $1,950 a month—50% of his PIA. Since this is less than her own benefit, she will not be able to claim an ex-spousal benefit on Peter's record. However, it's important for her to understand this fact.

- Second, she needs to be aware of and plan for the impact on her taxes. Social Security benefits are subject to ordinary income taxes. Depending on how much Patricia earns from her job, up to 85% of her Social Security benefit may be taxed as ordinary income.

- Third, she needs to consider her health insurance from work. If she has chosen a high-deductible health plan and is contributing to a Health Savings Account (HSA), she may want to delay starting Social Security. When you claim Social Security at or after age 65, Medicare Part A is automatically started. Social Security and Part A are bundled together, and you cannot decouple them. There is no monthly premium for Part A, so this is often not a big deal. However, if Patricia is contributing to an HSA, she must stop before she was planning to do so. Contributions to an HSA are not permitted once you have any part of Medicare. Furthermore, she may need to withdraw 8 or 9 months of contributions now deemed ineligible since Part A began retroactively.

- Fourth, she needs to consider the long-term effect of claiming before FRA. As a single person, she only has her own assets and income sources to rely on. If she can wait to claim at FRA, she will receive a higher amount for her entire retirement. And, importantly, Social Security's annual COLAs will be based on a larger benefit.

135

Since Patricia is still working, could she work for another year or two beyond FRA? For each year she delays claiming benefits after her FRA, up to age 70, she will receive an additional 8%. Even if she waits just one year until age 68 to claim, her monthly benefit will be 8% higher than at age 67. If she waits until age 70, her benefit will increase by 24%.

Her calculated benefit at FRA is $2,000. Waiting until 70 provides her with an additional $480 per month. That is a significant difference, especially for someone who must rely solely on her own resources to create and maintain a retirement paycheck.

The bottom line is that many questions need to be asked and answered before Patricia can decide the best claiming strategy for her now and in the future.

What about Peter and his Social Security benefits?

Like many divorced individuals in opposite-sex marriages, Peter was the higher earner. His PIA is estimated at $3,900 per month. Although he also meets all the rules as a divorced person, he will not be eligible to receive any ex-spousal benefits. His own benefit is considerably higher than 50% of Patricia's PIA of $2,000.

The adjustments to his own benefit will therefore be based only on his claiming decisions:

- If he claims before his own FRA, he will receive a reduction in monthly benefits and will be subject to the earnings limit if he is still working.

- If he claims after his FRA, he'll receive a boost with delayed retirement credits of up to 8% per year until age 70.

- His Social Security benefits will be taxed based on his overall income sources.

He does not lose any of his earned benefits because Patricia is also claiming and may be eligible for a small ex-spousal top-up as the lower earner.

Furthermore, Peter's second wife is not affected by Patricia's claiming situation at all. She will be independently considered for her own possible benefits. If she is a dependent spouse, she will be eligible for 50% of his PIA at her FRA. If she also receives her own worker benefits, she will receive her own benefits. If her own benefit is less than 50% of his PIA, her total benefit may include a spousal top-up.

The way the laws are written for divorced and remarried individuals protects benefits for all parties. There is no cut or reduction in benefits to the higher earner when multiple lower earners claim on their record. It's already built into the math.

Summary

Patricia's question about claiming Social Security benefits while working clearly shows how a simple question about Social Security benefits can lead to complicated issues. It highlights the system's complexity and how Social Security attempts to accommodate personal life situations.

If you are divorced, you may have the same options as Patricia. Keep in mind that once you claim, you usually make an irrevocable decision. You don't want to regret claiming early in your 80s or 90s.

You can claim your full, unreduced Social Security benefit the month you reach your FRA, even if you continue working full- or part-time and earn any amount of money.

If you meet the requirements for ex-spouses, you may qualify for ex-spousal benefits of up to 50% of your ex's full retirement benefit once you reach your FRA.

You can wait until age 70 to claim your own worker benefits. Only worker benefits can increase by an additional 8% per year through delayed retirement credits. Ex-spousal top-ups are not eligible for delayed retirement credits.

Remember that any Social Security benefit you receive counts as income. During your working years, it is more likely that part of your Social Security benefit will be subject to ordinary income tax.

CHAPTER 17:

Married for Years, then Divorced – Delighted to Claim on Her Ex

Every now and then, a woman leaves a lasting impression because her outlook on life is so positive. Deborah was 65 when I met her. She attended a Social Security presentation I gave in California. Afterwards, she waited in line for a long time to ask me a question about her situation.

She was married for many years before her divorce. She had started reading about Social Security and thought she read that she could claim a benefit based on her ex-spouse's work record. That seemed a little unusual to her, so she attended the workshop. We chatted afterwards, and I assured her that if his benefit was significantly higher than hers, she could likely claim on his record.

One year later...

The following year, I was invited back to California to once again lead a workshop on Social Security. Much to my surprise, Deborah was back. "You can never get enough information about Social Security," she commented. She had come back to the workshop to update me on her situation.

She visited her local Social Security office after the first workshop. The Social Security agent ran the numbers for her claiming options. Since she was not yet at her Full Retirement Age

SOCIAL SECURITY: LIGHTLY TOASTED, NOT BURNT

(FRA), she could either:

- Claim a reduced benefit then, or
- Wait to claim at FRA for her full benefit.

In either case, her benefit would include a sizeable ex-spousal top-up based on her ex's record!

Deborah was very surprised to see the difference between her calculated benefit and the amount on her statement. There was a large gap between Deborah's and her ex-husband's earning histories: his Primary Insurance Amount (PIA) was just over $4,000, and hers was about $950 per month.

They had two daughters together. Deborah spent over twenty years at home raising their girls. Overall, she has twenty-four years with no earnings on her record, and only recently earned her 40 credits. She mentioned that her first job was in 1977 when she was earning the minimum wage of $1.25 an hour. Many of her early working years contained low wages, so her own work record resulted in only a modest monthly benefit. Learning now that she's eligible for ex-spousal benefits will significantly improve her retirement income and her retirement lifestyle.

More to understand

Deborah had a big decision to make. Did she want to claim her newfound larger benefit now at age 66, before her FRA, with a reduced monthly payment? Or should she wait until FRA to claim?

Initially, she thought she could only receive $950 a month once she reached FRA. That's what her statement showed based on her work history. But then she learned that she'll receive her $950 plus an additional $1,050 in ex-spousal top-up benefits, totaling $2,000. But only if she waits until age 67, her FRA.

If she claims early at age 66, she will forfeit some monthly income because she will be claiming 12 months earlier. She would receive about $1,850 if she claims a year before her FRA, which is a 7.5% reduction.

Even though she'd lose some monthly benefits by claiming at 66 instead of 67, it's still significantly more than she ever expected to receive. $1,850 versus $950. And she might face a temporary clawback for some months while she is still working. But that is short-term thinking.

When Deborah spoke with me again after the second presentation, we discussed how deciding when to claim is truly a long-term decision. What she decides now at 66 will stick with her throughout her 80s and 90s. The decision not only affects her monthly cash flow but also sets her initial monthly payment, which becomes the foundation for all future cost-of-living adjustments.

She did like thinking long term and did not want to claim her benefit yet. With this new-found income, she really wants to maximize it the best she can. Since she's doing fine financially with her job now, she's focusing on the longer-term and planning to wait until FRA before claiming.

Why not wait until 70?

Her last question was why shouldn't she wait until age 70 to claim Social Security? She understands she can receive more from delayed retirement credits if she waits. Yes, workers can get a higher benefit by waiting to claim their own benefit until age 70. But the delayed retirement credits only apply to the worker's benefits, not to spousal or ex-spousal top-ups. She would not get an 8% per year increase on the full $2,000 benefit. She would only get 8% per year on her own $950 monthly benefit.

But if she chooses to do that, it simply means her ex-spousal top-up will be less than $1,050. Ex-spousal benefits are locked in based on the ex's PIA. According to her ex's PIA, her maximum benefit is $2,000 per month. If she receives more from her own benefit, she'll get less of a top-up. She will still end up with $2,000. It's just that the source of income shifts from one bucket to another. In her case, there is no point in waiting to claim after FRA.

Claiming on your ex is a private matter

One of the things Deborah told me after the second workshop was that she heard me loud and clear when I said that ex-spouses do not need to discuss their Social Security claiming options with their ex. They do not ask permission from their ex; they do not discuss their plans beforehand. The claiming decision is strictly between Social Security and the individual divorced person.

Well, Deborah told me she took a different path. She picked up the phone as soon as she got home from the Social Security office and called her ex-husband! She gleefully reported that she would be receiving more Social Security than she expected, based on his work history. She couldn't have been more delighted to share this new finding with him. Although she asked him why he didn't earn more while working, so she could have had an even higher benefit. Deborah is clearly a woman in charge and has a great sense of humor.

What will her ex-husband's benefits be?

Her ex remarried sometime after their divorce, so he cannot claim on Deborah's work record. Not to mention, his benefit is much higher than hers, so he wasn't eligible for ex-spousal top-up benefits anyway.

During her call, he mentioned that he claimed his own benefit early. His second wife is older than him, and they decided to retire when he turned 64. He wanted to capture the benefits he had already earned while he was younger. He was willing to accept a lower monthly payment.

His decision to claim early does not affect Deborah's maximum ex-spousal benefit. The calculation is still based on his original PIA, not the amount he is currently receiving. However, if he dies before Deborah, she will be able to change her claim to that of a divorced ex-spouse, and her benefits will increase to the amount he had been receiving at the time of his death. It would be better for both Deborah and his second wife if he had been receiving a larger benefit. Nevertheless, Deborah will be able to step into his shoes and claim a higher benefit in this situation.

Is it time to retire?

Deborah is trying to decide when to retire. She lives in a small guest house at one of her daughters' homes, so she doesn't have to worry about housing costs in retirement. And if she works for two more years, she'll qualify for a small income from her employer's private pension plan.

She has five wonderful grandchildren, ranging in ages from 3 to 17. She really wants to spend more time with them. She's also eager to travel around the US in a new car. She's confident she can afford a new car now that she knows about her increased income funded by her ex-spousal benefits.

Deborah may want to do some part-time work, or she may want to fully retire. She's taking her time to weigh her options. And, while she's still working, she's still increasing her Social Security benefits. All in all, she's doing an excellent job researching her options, learning more about ex-spousal benefits, and making sure to maximize this very important source of income for her retirement years. She is simply delighted to have learned she will be entitled to such a boost in Social Security income from those years she was married to her ex.

Summary

There were two critical steps that Deborah took when figuring out her Social Security options:

- She started researching her options well before reaching her FRA.
- She met with the Social Security Administration in person to get a look at her options.

And remember, there's no need to let your ex know that you're claiming on their record – unless you just want to rub it in!

SECTION 2D
Surviving Spouses Overview

CHAPTER 18:

Becoming a Widow or Widower

Much has been written about the dual dilemma of being a woman married to a man: Women often live significantly longer than their husbands, yet their lifetime earnings tend to be lower. Before Social Security, a woman dependent on her husband's retirement benefits could be left without income if he died first.

Social Security addressed the issue of widowhood early in the law's drafting. The lawmakers included specific provisions allowing widows to continue receiving Social Security benefits after their husbands' deaths. However, wives do not always outlive their husbands.

Initially, men who became widowers did not receive surviving spouse benefits. Most often, this was irrelevant because the wife had no earnings or Social Security benefits on her own record. Over time, that situation changed. Some men could benefit from higher Social Security benefits based on their deceased wife's record.

It took until the 1970s for Social Security to eliminate this gender bias. In one of Ruth Bader Ginsburg's signature arguments before the Supreme Court, she argued that a woman's earnings should be considered equal in value to a man's earnings. Therefore, a widower raising his wife's children should be entitled to survivor benefits. Similarly, a husband with a lower retirement benefit should be able to receive his wife's higher retirement benefit as a widower.

Surviving spouse situations are complex

Thinking back to America between the 1930s and 1970s, the country was thriving on jobs in manufacturing, coal mining, and industrial work. It was an era when "heavy lifting" jobs were the norm. The chances of a male worker dying from his job were high; therefore, many widows were left to fend for themselves. Women often became widows at a young age while raising children or early in their retirement.

The average life expectancy in the US in 1940 was 62 for white males and 52 for black males. By 1950, white males lived on average to 67, but black males only to 59. Women lived about five years longer on average.

So, how should Social Security handle widowhood? What about young mothers left to raise their children? Social Security retirement benefits are meant for retirement; but if a husband dies at 50, then what? Does a widow with children at home go without any income for 15 years? Of course, that made no sense.

General provisions for widows

The lawmakers at the time looked at the situations surrounding widowhood and included provisions based first on the relative eligibility of the worker and then on the widow's age. For example, if the worker was 65 or older and receiving retirement benefits, his widow would "step into his shoes" and receive the same amount, but only if she were of retirement age – 65 or older.

If she had not yet reached Full Retirement Age (FRA), she could receive a reduced widow's benefit as early as age 60.

But what would happen to a younger woman who becomes a widow? What if she hadn't yet reached age 60? In this case, the assumption was made that she would have access to savings or life insurance, or that she would still be young enough to find work that would provide her with at least a basic income. She may have to make serious trade-offs and wouldn't necessarily be as comfortable as when her husband was alive. But the Social Security law specifically addressed women in their old age (retirement) and if they became a young widow while raising children.

These provisions and rules are still in place today. The only addition is that the law now includes benefits for men who become widowers, whether in old age or when they are younger and raising young children.

Calculating benefits for widows(ers) with children

In the late 1930s, Congress needed to decide how to provide for survivors when a young woman raising a worker's children became a widow. The protections under Social Security needed to be broad enough to address real situations that can happen to a worker's family.

In the case of a young mother becoming a widow, she would receive a surviving spouse benefit equal to 75% of her husband's eligible payment amount until their youngest child reached age 16. Additionally, any minor child would also receive benefit payments of 75% of their father's eligible benefit amount until they reached age 18, or 19 if still in high school. If there are several children in the household, there will be an overall family maximum, so some adjustments to prorate payments may occur.

These family rules applied to all widows raising deceased workers' children. Sadly, some women become widows at age 28 when their children are all under five years old. Sometimes a wife becomes a widow at 48 with three high schoolers. Social Security survivor benefits were created to help in these situations. Widows have found this safety net to be very helpful during times of great personal loss and often significant financial hardship.

Again, it wasn't until the 1970s that young fathers raising the deceased mother's children became eligible for survivor benefits. In reality, it may be that the widowed young father never receives these survivor benefits while his children are minors. More often, he will continue to work, and his earnings will likely exceed the earnings limit. However, his minor children would still be entitled to survivor benefits.

Funeral directors play a key role with Social Security

If you've never planned a funeral before, you might not know that the funeral director will ask for the deceased person's Social Security number. Why? It's because the funeral director immediately contacts Social Security to report the death and provide any information about a surviving spouse and children.

Since the death of a spouse can be a particularly difficult time, having someone notify Social Security that updates are needed can be very helpful. Usually, a Social Security representative will reach out to the surviving spouse and arrange any available payments. This ensures the surviving spouse and minor children receive the correct income.

If a retiree dies at an older age, the funeral director also contacts Social Security on their behalf. This ensures that payments to the deceased stop timely, preventing the need to recover any ineligible payments made to the deceased person.

If there is an overpayment, meaning the deceased continued to receive payments after death, it will be the widow's or widower's responsibility to return the excess amounts. No one wants to deal with that on top of everything else happening in the first months after losing a spouse. (If there is no surviving spouse, the estate would need to pay back any ineligible amounts received.)

Special provisions for widows(ers)

Where the law recognizes the potential financial hardships faced by widows and now widowers, it allows for earlier access to surviving spousal (or surviving ex-spousal) retirement benefits. Instead of waiting until age 62 to claim, a widow or widower can start survivor benefits as early as age 60. Additionally, the survivor FRA may be slightly younger than the retirement FRA.

Perhaps most importantly, the law established survivor benefits as a separate tranche from regular retirement benefits. This allows a surviving spouse to maximize monthly payments at different ages, and it enables them to switch between tranches if it results in a higher payment.

The FRA to access unreduced survivor benefits is shown in the following table. Like with figuring out your own worker FRA, it depends on the year you were born.

Year You Were Born	Full Retirement Age (FRA)	Survivor Full Retirement Age (S-FRA)
1945 - 1954 (different from FRA table)	66	66
1955	66 and 2 months	66
1956	66 and 4 months	66
1957	66 and 6 months	66 and 2 months
1958	66 and 8 months	66 and 4 months
1959	66 and 10 months	66 and 6 months
1960	67	66 and 8 months
1961	67	66 and 10 months
1962 and later	67	67

How do survivor benefits work in real life?

Let's look at the options Sally Snowflake will have if she out-lives her husband Richard Raine. She was born in 1961. There-fore, her Survivor FRA is 66 years and 10 months, and her own FRA is at age 67. Let's assume she did not have her own work record. Therefore, she'll be eligible to receive a full retirement spousal benefit when she reaches her FRA—50% of Richard's PIA. If Richard claims at his FRA and is receiving $2,000 per month, Sally's spousal benefit is $1,000.

Depending on Sally's age when Richard dies, she will have different benefit options. Let's first explore the possibilities if Sally is between 60 and 67 years old when Richard dies:

- If Sally had not yet claimed her spousal benefit, it disappears when Richard dies. She will then only qualify for a surviving spouse benefit. She can choose to start her survivor benefit immediately or wait until she reaches her Survivor FRA of 66 and 10 months. Claiming before S-FRA results in a reduced payment. Waiting until S-FRA allows her to receive the maximum amount she is eligible for.

- If she had already claimed her spousal benefit before Richard died, her spousal benefit will automatically switch to her surviving spouse benefit. This will give her a higher payment, but her own spousal benefit will stop. If she is younger than her FRA, her survivor benefits will be reduced because she has not yet reached her S-FRA.

Now, let's see what options Sally has if she is well into retire-ment—around age 80—when Richard dies. In this case, she will step into his shoes and automatically start receiving his higher payment. There will be no reduction since she is well over her S-FRA. After years of receiving annual cost-of-living adjustments, assume Richard's original $2,000 per month benefit has increased to $3,400. Sally steps into the $3,400 per month, but she loses her initial $1,000 spousal benefit.

The following table summarizes the different options available to a spouse when becoming a surviving spouse at various ages.

Sally's Age when Richard Dies	Her Spousal Benefit...	Her Surviving Spouse Benefits...	Considerations
Age 60...	Does not apply She's not yet 62, so she cannot yet access the spousal benefit	$1,430 She can choose to claim a reduced survivor benefit as early as 60 (at a 28.5% reduction)	Reduced surviving spouse benefits begin at age 60. Full survivor benefits are only paid once she reaches her S-FRA.
Age 62 and already claimed her spousal benefit...	$650 She was collecting a spousal benefit reduced by 35% due to early claiming	$1,580 Her spousal benefit will end, and reduced survivor benefits will begin	At 62, Sally claimed her spousal benefit since Richard had already filed. When he died, she automatically switched to her survivor benefit. Any claim before her FRA will be reduced.
Age 67 and claimed her spousal benefit... (66 and 10 months is her surviving spouse FRA)	$1,000 She'll receive her full 50% of his PIA spousal benefit	$2,000 Her spousal benefit will end, and she will automatically step into his shoes and receive the full payment he was getting	Now that Sally has reached her own FRA, she's reached the maximum amount of benefits she will be entitled to, both as a dependent spouse eligible for spousal benefits and as a surviving spouse.
Age 70 and claimed at her FRA	$1,000 Spousal benefits do not increase with delayed retirement credits. They automatically stop when Richard dies	$2,154 (his benefit has increased with annual COLAs) She will automatically step into his shoes and receive the same amount he had been getting	There is no reason for Sally to wait until 70 to claim her spousal benefit. Her maximum payments were available to her at her FRA. Her benefits will automatically switch to survivor benefits upon Richard's death.

What if a survivor has their own work record?

When a surviving spouse is between 60 and 70 years old and has their own work record, they have three buckets to juggle to figure out when their ultimate highest monthly benefit becomes available. Will it be

- Their own worker benefit at FRA or age 70?
- Their spousal benefit (maximum amount 50% of their spouse's PIA)?
- Their surviving spouse benefit at S-FRA?

It is important to plan for widowhood early in the retirement income planning process. This ensures each person knows which strategy provides the highest Social Security income and when. Consider the best approach for each person, including situations where one outlives the other.

Let's revisit Sally and Richard. Assume the same situation for Richard as in the previous example: his PIA is $2,000 per month. Sally's spousal maximum is therefore $1,000 per month. But now, suppose Sally also worked, and her own benefit is $2,400 per month, which is higher than half of Richard's PIA. What will her options be for claiming Social Security if she becomes a widow?

Since her own benefit is higher than her spousal benefit ($2,400 versus $1,000), she will not be eligible for a spousal benefit, so that option is off the table. Her Social Security payment options will be based on her own work history and her survivor benefits. The following table outlines several situations.

Sally's Age	Her Own Benefit	Her Surviving Spouse Benefits	Considerations
60	N/A She's not yet 62, so she cannot access retirement benefits based on her own work record	$1,430 She can begin benefits at a 28.5% reduction	If Sally needed income, she could claim as a surviving spouse starting at age 60, but at a reduced amount.
62	$1,680 A 30% reduction due to early claiming	$1,580 Reduced survivor benefits are available between age 60 and FRA	At 62, Sally is now eligible to claim either her own retirement benefits or her survivor benefits. These benefits are reduced if claimed early.
67 (66 and 10 months is her S- FRA)	$2,400 Her full benefit amount	$2,000 At her survivor FRA, she's eligible to step into his shoes and receive the full payment he was receiving	At Sally's FRA, she has reached the maximum amount of her surviving spouse benefits. Her own benefit is higher than her survivor benefit, so she should choose the survivor benefit and let her own grow until age 70.
70	$2,970 Her own worker benefits increase 8% per year between FRA and age 70	$2,000 Survivor benefits do not increase after the worker dies, except for annual COLAs	At age 70, Sally's benefit has increased by 24%. It is significantly higher than Richard's PIA at the time of his death. Therefore, waiting until age 70 to claim her own benefit maximizes her income during her later years.

For someone in a similar situation, where both spouses have their own significant work records, it's generally advisable to claim surviving spouse benefits first at S-FRA. Or claim them earlier even if they will be reduced. This approach allows the surviving spouse's own work benefit to grow to the maximum possible amount at age 70.

However, if claiming either benefit before FRA, the earnings limit will apply. So, if the surviving spouse is still working, they may not receive any Social Security payments until FRA. (More on the earnings limit in Part 3.)

What's important to understand is that when you become a widow or widower, you might have two "buckets" of Social Security income to consider. When a surviving spouse qualifies for these benefits, choosing the option that provides the larger payment at the time of claiming may be the best choice. Or, it could be better to accept a lower benefit for a few years and then switch to the other that offers a higher benefit later in life.

Household income falls for widows and widowers

It is important for married couples to plan for the period after one spouse passes away. For those already receiving Social Security retirement benefits, household income will drop significantly when the first spouse dies. Not planning ahead can result in an unwanted and unexpected surprise.

Social Security payments stop the month the first spouse dies. This means if your spouse dies on March 19th, their benefits end that day. Both February payments will be deposited in March since both were alive for the entire month of February.

Starting with the April payment, the surviving spouse will receive only one benefit. If the survivor was receiving the smaller amount, they will now get the larger one as their sole monthly benefit. Usually, the survivor should expect about one-third to one-half less than what both spouses previously received. This can significantly impact household finances.

Take a look at a few examples for Sally and Richard, who were both collecting benefits before he died. Regardless of how much Sally had been receiving as a spouse or on her own record, once Richard dies, the overall household income drops significantly – even if her survivor benefit turns out to be higher than her own benefit had been.

	Sally's Benefit Payment	Richard's Benefit Payment	Total Household Income from Social Security	% Reduction After Richard's Death
Both are alive	$1,000	$2,000	$3,000	n/a
After Richard's death	$2,000	n/a	$2,000	-33%

	Sally's Benefit Payment	Richard's Benefit Payment	Total Household Income from Social Security	% Reduction After Richard's Death
Both are alive	$2,400	$2,000	$4,400	n/a
After Richard's death	$2,400	n/a	$2,400	-45%

	Sally's Benefit Payment	Richard's Benefit Payment	Total Household Income from Social Security	% Reduction After Richard's Death
Both are alive	$1,800	$1,800	$3,600	n/a
After Richard's death	$1,800	n/a	$1,800	-50%

It is critically important to remember this fact and plan for a significant drop in income from Social Security. The reality is that when your spouse dies, your household will not pay much less in living expenses. In fact, it is rare that costs drop significantly at all. The lights need to stay on, and the surviving spouse still needs to eat. Additionally, taxes may increase substantially as the survivor now files as an individual. Furthermore, Medicare Part B premiums may also increase when becoming an individual tax filer.

Carefully planning how the survivor will make up for lost Social Security income is a critical task in retirement income planning.

Ex-wives can often claim as survivors, but less common for ex-husbands

The Social Security law addresses what happens to benefits for ex-wives. If you meet the eligibility rules as a qualifying ex-spouse (see previous chapters), you also qualify for survivor benefits. If you were married to your ex-spouse for 10 or more years before the divorce, you are generally eligible for surviving ex-spouse benefits if they die first. If you are eligible to receive a higher monthly check by stepping into your deceased ex's shoes, you should do so.

In this situation, unlike for married couples, it is unlikely that a funeral director will inform Social Security that the deceased has an ex-wife. Therefore, it will be your responsibility to contact Social Security when you learn that your ex has died. They will need documentation that proves your marriage to your ex and the divorce decree. Afterward, they will review all your options and help ensure that you receive the highest possible monthly income.

In most cases, only an ex-wife qualifies to collect ex-spousal survivor benefits, because she often has lower Social Security benefits. However, this is not always the case. Some ex-husbands find out their ex-wives had higher benefits. He must provide proof of marriage and divorce, but once verified, he might be able to switch to surviving ex-spousal benefits and start receiving a higher monthly benefit.

Although that was not how the law was originally written, it is now. Therefore, unmarried ex-spouses, regardless of gender, should contact the SSA to see if they qualify for a higher benefit. Ex-spouses who remarried after age 60 might also be eligible for a higher benefit based on their deceased ex's record. It can't hurt to making a phone call, even if your ex passed away several years ago.

For same-sex married couples, the same rules apply

If you become a widow when your same-sex spouse dies, the same rules for stepping into their shoes apply. Since same-sex marriages were legalized at the federal level in 2015, the same rights and benefits that apply to opposite-sex marriages also apply to same-sex marriages.

When the first spouse dies, the surviving spouse or surviving ex-spouse is entitled to have their Social Security benefits reviewed and considered if a larger monthly payment is available.

The same age rules also apply. If you were the spouse who stayed home to raise the children, or if your own Primary Insurance Amount is less than what you will receive as a spouse, you become eligible for spousal benefits based on the higher earning spouse's work record once you reach age 62. You become eligible for survivor spouse benefits once you reach age 60. And, if you are a young widow(er) raising the children you had with your deceased spouse, you and your children are entitled to family benefits. Your survivor benefits will continue until your youngest child reaches age 16, but the child's benefits continue until they graduate from high school at age 18 or 19.

If you're unsure whether any of the surviving spouse rules apply to you, contact Social Security to confirm.

Working and claiming can eliminate some benefits

One area of Social Security survivor rules that surprises many is the coordination between current work wages and collecting survivor benefits when you are younger than FRA (more information on the earnings limit test in Part 3). If you become a widow(er) and claim Social Security benefits while also working for a covered employer, you can expect a reduction in benefits until you reach your FRA.

The typical question I get is something like this: "I'm 58 and a widow. I heard I can start getting survivor benefits at age 60. Is that correct?"

Before answering, I need to ask if they are still working. If they are, I explain that while they can continue to work and claim survivor benefits at 60, their benefits will be reduced – and possibly eliminated entirely – if their salary is higher than about $20,000.

Keep in mind that survivor benefits are designed to provide income for a surviving spouse during their retirement years. Only when a surviving spouse reaches FRA does Social Security consider them retired. That means the surviving spouse can work and receive full survivor benefits without any reduction once they reach FRA.

But the earning limit test applies all the way to FRA. So a younger surviving spouse who is eligible to collect benefits could lose them if their job pays significantly more than the earnings limit. And an older surviving spouse might also have some months where no Social Security is paid. All of this changes once the survivor reaches FRA.

The earnings limit test does not stop at Survivor FRA. So, there may be a two- or four-month gap when the earnings limit still applies to survivor benefits. It might not cause a clawback, but it could, depending on your exact salary.

Upon reaching FRA, survivor benefits are paid in full, even if the widow(er) continues to work. This strategy allows surviving spouses to claim a survivor benefit while their own benefit increases with delayed retirement credits. However, before reaching FRA, any benefit, including survivor benefits, gets clawed back if the survivor earns too much money.

Surviving spouse benefits and remarriage

One last note about becoming a widow or widower. In general, you qualify for survivor spouse benefits if you were married to your spouse for at least nine months. However, if your spouse dies in an accident or while serving in the military, the nine-month rule is waived.

What if you became a young widow or widower and later re-married? You would not be eligible for surviving spouse benefits if you remarried before turning 60. However, if your second spouse also dies before you, you again become a surviving spouse. In this case, you will be eligible to step into the shoes of either spouse number one or spouse number two – whichever had the higher benefit amount.

On the other hand, if a surviving spouse remarries after age 60, they can claim surviving spouse benefits. Later, they might receive a higher monthly income from their new spouse with a spousal benefit. Or they can switch to their own benefit later if it is the larger one.

If you think these rules are rather complex, you'd be in good company. The main thing to remember is that if you become a widow or widower, contact Social Security. The agents will help you determine which records you are eligible to claim on, and which option will give you the highest monthly payment at that time.

However, before claiming either benefit, it's critical to consult with a financial advisor who specializes in Social Security surviving spouse strategies. Each survivor will have a different best strategy based on their personal circumstances at the time of their spouse's death. Don't feel pressured to decide quickly; you have up to six months to make a decision. Social Security can pay benefits retroactively for up to six months from the date you contact them.

Learn from married couples who have traveled this road

In the following chapters, you'll meet two women who became widows at different times. You can download a checklist and action plan on my blog: https://boomerretirementbriefs.com.

Read on to see how important Social Security is for women who became widows.

- Mary lost her first husband when her children were young. She later remarried and then divorced her second husband. After her second husband's death, she received a surprising increase in income.

- Gail got it all right when she married her second husband. He was the love of her life. Eleven months into her retirement, he was diagnosed with cancer. Two months later, she became a widow.

CHAPTER 19:

Married, Early Widowhood, Remarried, Divorced, Surviving Ex-Spouse

Marriage starts out so hopeful and we look forward to building a life and family with the partner we choose. Mary waited a long time to find the right guy. Donny was all she could have hoped for. She was an older bride, so as soon as they said their "I do's," they started a family. Within three years, they had two beautiful children. And life was good. Mary worked with children with disabilities. She loved her job but happily gave it up to stay home and raise her children. Donny worked for a large retail store. There were family picnics, vacations to the shore, and special time every night reading to the children.

Then a call came from the hospital. Donny had been in an accident, and Mary should come immediately. He didn't survive. Mary went from her idyllic life to being a widow with two young children in the blink of an eye. Her world fell apart.

Getting on new financial footing

There was a small amount of life insurance, enough to pay off the mortgage. Donny's army pension provided a modest income. But it was Social Security that helped her keep food on the table during those first difficult years.

As the surviving spouse raising Donny's children, Mary was eligible for survivor benefits before age 60. Each child also received a monthly benefit. They were four and two when Donny died, so their payments would continue for many years. Mary received 75% of Donny's calculated benefit at the time of his death. Each of the children also received 75% of his calculated benefit, adjusted to the family maximum at that time.

After the first year of adjusting to being a single parent, Mary knew it was time to return to her career. She found a job working at a local school. This provided a substantial salary for her, and she worked "school hours," so she was home in the afternoons with her children. However, because she was working and earning more than the earnings limit allowed for full payment of her survivor benefits, her benefits were clawed back. The children's benefits were not affected.

Getting remarried

Fast forward several years, and Mary met Nicholas. He was eight years older, had lost his first wife some years earlier, and his children were grown and living on their own. They decided to marry. She was 50 and he was 58. Since Mary remarried before turning 60, any survivor benefits she might qualify for were discontinued. However, the children's benefits continued until they each reached age 18.

Unfortunately, after 12 years of marriage, Mary and Nicholas decided to divorce. At this point, Mary was 62. She found that she was eligible for three possible claiming categories:

- Her own Social Security retirement benefit based on her work history.
- As a surviving spouse with benefits based on her first husband Donny's record.
- As a qualifying ex-spouse on her ex-husband Nicholas' record.

Another new financial situation to set up

Mary was still working in the school district. She had some decisions to make about whether to continue working, which benefit to claim, and when. Since she qualified for both retirement and survivor benefits, she could claim one benefit early and wait until FRA or later for the other.

If she claimed any benefit at 62, it would be reduced because she's claiming before FRA. In addition, depending on the earnings limit, some or all of her benefits could be clawed back.

If she claimed either her own or her ex-spousal benefit, whichever was higher, she could switch at her Full Retirement Age (FRA) to her surviving spouse benefit if it were the highest benefit.

She knew Nicholas' PIA was the highest among the options, so if he died before she did, she would eventually step into his shoes and receive a higher benefit.

The first decision she made was to continue working. She enjoyed working with the children and wanted to stay busy during the day. Her income far exceeds the earnings limit on Social Security, so she would not request payments until her FRA. The following table outlines Mary's most likely estimates when she claims her benefits.

A look at the many options available

Mary can claim various benefits at different ages. (All estimates are approximate and rounded.)

Benefit Type	Mary's Monthly Benefit	Donny's Calculated Benefit	Nicholas' Benefit
Primary Insurance Amount (PIA)	$1,600 On her own work record	$1,200 Locked in when he died so early	$3,600 His PIA and the amount he received when he claimed
Ex-spousal Benefit at FRA (maximum potential)	$1,800 includes a $200 top-up on Nicholas' work record		
Surviving Spouse Benefit at S-FRA	$1,200 On Donny's history		
Survivor Benefit if Nicholas dies before Mary	$3,600 Possible amount based on Nicholas' history		
Mary's age 70 benefit amount from her own record	$1,980 After delayed retirement credits are applied		

Mary's goal was to maximize her Social Security benefits, especially in her later years. Since she only depended on herself to manage her retirement income, the choices she made were crucial to her future financial well-being. After reviewing the numbers, she planned the following:

- At FRA, she's eligible for a maximum of $1,800 as an ex-spouse or a $1,200 surviving spouse benefit on Donny's record. If she claims her ex-spousal benefit, she is deemed to file for both her own benefit ($1,600) plus her ex-spousal top up ($200). It may seem obvious to claim the ex-spousal benefit...

- ...but she first needs to consider what happens to her benefit at age 70. Waiting until age 70 results in a slightly higher income based on Mary's work record. Her own maximum benefit of $1,980 is higher than her ex-spousal benefit on Nicholas's record ($1,800), and also higher than her survivor benefit on Donny's record ($1,200).

The goal is to focus on her single highest benefit possible for her long retirement. If Mary claims at her FRA, she needs to keep in mind that her highest benefit is her own at age 70. To get that amount, she cannot first claim ex-spousal benefits, as they come from the same "bucket." She can only switch between survivor benefits and her own benefits (a combination of her work record plus the extra ex-spousal top-up).

While Nicholas is still alive, her best option is to claim her survivor benefit at FRA and then switch to her own age 70 benefit three years later.

Later, if Nicholas dies before her, she could step into his shoes and receive $3,600 per month. In fact, this was the case. At age 80, Mary learned that Nicholas had died. She met with Social Security with proper documentation. They switched her benefit from her own retirement benefit at age 70 to her survivor benefit based on her ex-husband's record.

Summary

The rules for claiming benefits for widows or widowers with young children can be quite complicated. As long as they are eligible to claim on multiple people's records, those options stay open throughout their lives. The highest benefit, among those they are eligible for might not be the one they start with. In some cases, widows or widowers can switch from one benefit to another if it results in a higher monthly income.

It is clear how important Social Security was for Mary and her children. It truly was a saving grace after Donny died so unexpectedly, leaving her alone with two young children. Sadly, her second marriage didn't last; however, because it was a long-term marriage, it provided another record she might depend on for retirement benefits in her later years.

CHAPTER 20:

Retirement Plans Cut Suddenly and Unfairly Short

It takes years to plan the perfect retirement. And when everything begins to come together exactly as planned, excitement grows. Gail and Bruce had been preparing for their retirement for years. They planned and plotted how they would spend their days by the pool, enjoying their ever-growing brood of grandchildren, and sipping bourbon cocktails.

Gail was an executive at a large company for 25 years. When she announced her retirement, it was met with hearty congratulations. Gail's plan for retirement included working until her Full Retirement Age (FRA) so she could gracefully close her career chapter and joyfully begin her retirement years. Her financial plan was set, and she was prepared for this new phase. Let the celebration begin!

It's party time

Gail and Bruce, who had retired several years earlier, kicked off their "official retirement" with a road trip to Florida. Instead of wintering up north, they moved for three months to southern Florida. Every morning, they had coffee on the lanai, watching the surf roll in. For eight weeks, they entertained small groups of family and long-time friends.

Week nine was declared "party week." They invited 30 of their closest friends to join them for a weekend at the beach and a special celebratory dinner at Gail's favorite five-star restaurant. It was quite a bash! And, for Gail and Bruce, it was the perfect way to mark this major milestone in their lives.

Sometimes, second time is the charm

For both of them, this was their second marriage. They each had two grown children and grandchildren from their respective families. They took special care of each other, having come from first marriages that were not ideal. The love and respect between them was evident in everything they did. It was a strong and powerful partnership.

Gail's first marriage lasted just over 10 years; Bruce's first marriage lasted 15. By the time of retirement, they had been together for 30 years and married for 25. There was travel on the horizon and finally the time to do whatever they wanted.

Retirement year one comes to a devastating close

Eleven months into Gail's retirement, Bruce was diagnosed with pancreatic cancer – inoperable, and the prognosis was grim. To say this was a shock does not even come close to describing what was happening in this family. It was utterly devastating.

They shared one final Christmas together. The four children, their spouses, and all the grandchildren gathered for a family celebration.

One year into Gail's retirement, the love of her life was gone. And her world stopped.

On becoming a widow

The shock of becoming a widow can bring even the strongest, most capable woman to her knees. On every front, there is something to handle, all while the grief remains overwhelming.

Fortunately, because Gail and Bruce had been planning for retirement for a long time, she was financially prepared. They had seven weeks together at the end, giving them time to make final decisions about their finances, the house, and the children.

Social Security retirement benefits were relatively straightforward for Gail. She claimed her own benefit a year earlier when she retired. It was a few months after reaching her Full Retirement Age. Bruce had retired early and claimed his benefit a couple of years before reaching his FRA.

They both had similar Primary Insurance Amounts based on their work histories. Their strategy was for Bruce to claim early and for Gail to claim at her FRA. Neither wanted to work until age 70, and they preferred not to tap into their hard-earned savings sooner than necessary. They each contributed to Social Security for 50 years. Now was the time to start their benefits and use them as the foundation of their retirement income.

When Bruce died, his benefit check stopped entirely. His payment was less than Gail's because he claimed before his FRA. Gail's payment continued to be deposited into her bank account, but her household income from Social Security dropped 40% when Bruce's check stopped. Social Security never missed a single payment, but it's still jarring when one check suddenly stops. The funeral director handled notifying Social Security that Bruce had died.

Was there another option?

Only if she had not yet filed a claim when Bruce died. In that case, Gail could have immediately stepped into Bruce's shoes. She would have received the monthly amount he had been getting as a surviving spouse benefit. Then, when she turned 70, she could have requested to switch to her own benefit, which would reach the maximum payout amount.

While this option might sound good in theory, it would mean that Gail would have to withdraw more income from her savings than she wanted during the first four years of her retirement. Keep in mind, Social Security cannot be passed on to your children or grandchildren. It's your personal savings that are passed to the beneficiaries of your choice. One of Gail and Bruce's goals was to leave a legacy to the grandchildren if possible.

Deciding when to claim Social Security involves weighing different options and understanding the trade-offs. This makes it easier to put a good plan in place for your retirement finances.

Summary

There is never a good time to become a widow or widower. It's especially cruel to face widowhood right at the start of retirement, after working so hard all those years. Not even getting a full year together, let alone five or 10, feels unbearable.

Gail had some invaluable advice to offer when planning for retirement. While it is aimed at women, it definitely applies to men too.

- Before retiring, get your financial ducks in a row.
- Make a plan and know where all your income will come from.
- If your spouse dies first, one Social Security check will stop. Know where you'll be making up that income.
- Know where the safety deposit key is. Know where every document is, where every dollar is.

This level of detailed financial planning requires a lot of time. Gail strongly recommends you dedicate the necessary time while you're together. It would be crushing to try to handle this at the same time you're also grieving the loss of your spouse.

Even as buttoned-up as Gail and Bruce were, some things still slipped through the cracks. She spent hours on the phone with a credit card company and switching insurance policies. These tasks are daunting and exhausting on a good day. When you are grieving, these tasks can feel insurmountable.

While it might seem unthinkable to plan for becoming a surviving spouse, the more you can prepare for this possibility, the less overwhelming it will be to handle the financial realities if you find yourself in that position. You'll need years to grieve and figure out what your new life will look like. Gail's advice is to give yourself the time and space to get your legs back on solid ground. Having your financials in order makes this unwanted journey a bit more secure.

SECTION 3:
More Social Security Must-Know Tips

CHAPTER 21:

Big Changes for Those Who Also Receive A Public Pension

What on earth are WEP (rhymes with "rep") and GPO? Teachers in 15 different states, workers in their town or city offices, police officers, firefighters, and many others who worked for their state or local governments in some capacity know about WEP and GPO, and – let me assure you – no one has been happy about these three-letter sections of Social Security law.

Let's start with WEP, which stands for the Windfall Elimination Provision. This is the part of the Social Security law that states if you receive certain types of public pension payments (those from your state or certain unions), and you also earned enough credits to qualify for Social Security on your own work record, you would not be eligible to receive the full Social Security benefit you see on your statement.

GPO stands for Government Pension Offset. It is a part of the Social Security law that impacts spousal benefits. GPO applies when someone receives a pension from a job with a state or local government and would normally qualify for a Social Security benefit as a spouse, ex-spouse, or surviving spouse. The public pension was intended to be their main retirement benefit. Benefits were accrued in a public pension plan instead of Social Security. As a result, Social Security spousal payments could be significantly reduced or even eliminated.

In January 2025, these two cut-back provisions were completely repealed by the 118th Congress, and President Biden signed the repeal into law. This was an unexpected standalone law called the Social Security Fairness Act. It went into effect in January 2024, a full year before it was officially enacted. The result was that about 3 million former public service workers received a significant boost in their retirement income, along with a check for up to 15 months of retroactive payments.

Some background

For decades, the Social Security Administration and Congress have known that Social Security would face challenges due to demographic shifts. There would be many more Social Security recipients than workers paying into the system when the Baby Boomers retired. Over the years, many ideas have been proposed to help stabilize this imbalance.

One of the identified problem areas was a particular group of employers: the states and unions that chose to fund their own pensions instead of contributing to Social Security. These are the "uncovered" employers. The arrangement was that state workers would receive a pension rather than Social Security.

In jobs where the individual states opted out of Social Security, the retirement benefits paid to retired employees were to be fair and comparable to what these workers would have received under Social Security. There should be no double-dipping of retirement benefits. Therefore, each worker either receives their own public pension or an earned Social Security benefit.

The WEP calculation

If someone spends their career in state government or teaching, and their only benefit is a pension, that is straightforward. At retirement, they will receive a monthly pension benefit.

But what happens when someone's work history includes a combination of jobs where sometimes they're eligible for a state pension and other times for Social Security benefits? The Social Security law addressed these workers by giving priority to the pension. These hybrid workers would receive their full pension benefit, and their Social Security benefit would be recalculated to reflect an adjusted covered earnings history. In other words, they'd usually receive a reduced Social Security benefit.

The reduction was calculated using a different Primary Insurance Amount (PIA) formula. Social Security considers all the years when a worker earned "substantial income" from a covered employer. However, a hybrid worker might have many years with zero earnings from uncovered work, which can make them appear to be a low-wage worker. As a result, their PIA could be artificially high. Therefore, the individual worker's recalculated benefit was adjusted to reflect that they primarily have a pension and are not a low-wage worker.

There is a short paragraph on all Social Security statements that warns workers that if they have a state pension, the estimate shown is probably incorrect. However, most people overlook this small paragraph.

In reality, hybrid workers typically receive a greater total benefit from their pension combined with reduced Social Security than they would from Social Security alone. And this "windfall" was deemed unfair by Congress back in 1983.

The GPO calculation

People also miss the sentence on their statements that says if they receive a state pension, any spousal or survivor benefits will be reduced. The coordination between teachers' unions or state pensions with Social Security exists to prevent individuals from receiving two large retirement benefits. If a public worker is receiving a substantial pension, they should not also be eligible for a significant spousal, ex-spousal, or survivor benefit.

Congress addressed this seemingly unfair advantage in 1977 by correcting the overpayments under the GPO. The law established a formula to reduce Social Security benefits: two-thirds of the monthly pension amount would be subtracted from any Social Security spousal, ex-spousal, or surviving spouse benefit. In many cases, these spousal benefits would be reduced to zero. This is rarely good news for a spouse, especially when they didn't realize that working for, say, 40 years at Town Hall or 35 years as a teacher in one of the 15 "special" pension states could significantly lower or eliminate their Social Security benefit as a spouse.

Again, the rationale here is that working for an employer with a retirement system in place of Social Security does not entitle that worker to a retirement payment significantly greater than what an at-home spouse would receive, which can be up to half of the spouse's PIA.

A change of heart?

So how is it that, out of the clear blue, Congress pushed through the Social Security Fairness Act, completely eliminating both of these reduction formulas? Did that particular Congress have a change of heart and become a kinder, gentler legislative body? Not exactly.

It is no secret in 2025 that the Social Security program needs to be shored up quickly. In order to pay fully earned benefits to all Baby Boomers, Gen Xers, and future generations, additional funding is essential. Since 1990, every Congress member has been aware of this impending issue. Innovative and new solutions are needed to guarantee the program's solvency and full benefit delivery.

So, increasing benefit payments for 3 million public workers seemed to push solvency in the wrong direction. However, most Americans didn't realize that police and fire unions had been lobbying for the last 40 years! A core group has been fighting against the unfairness of WEP and GPO. These provisions are especially harmful to those in physically demanding safety and first responder careers. Police and fire workers often must retire in their early to late 50s. They don't just sit on the couch at that point and do nothing. Instead, they take on new jobs with covered employers.

We have a tremendous need for workers, and they need a paycheck. As a result, hybrid careers are common. If you earn enough credits for a Social Security benefit and have fairly paid into the system, you should be entitled to your calculated benefit without any restrictions.

That message finally got through to Congress, and they agreed. Going forward, WEP and GPO are fully repealed. Although there was a small but significant impact on the Social Security reserve account, many believe this was the right and fair decision. And now, it is the law.

A note about other pensions

Many retirees often receive two retirement payments: their full Social Security retirement benefit and their complete pension. Why does this happen? How can it be fair?

People who worked for many large corporations often had a defined benefit pension plan as part of their benefits packages. In addition, the employer was a covered employer, so their wages up to the taxable wage base were subject to FICA.

It's not unfair in these situations—there are simply two distinct benefits because that's what the employer set up and paid into. Decisions about how to design benefits packages are made by professional benefits managers. Each company decides whether to offer a pension plan in addition to paying into FICA for Social Security. When payments are made into two plans, retirement benefits are paid to eligible employees from both plans.

Read more about WEP and GPO

Visit https://boomerretirementbriefs.com to learn more about the repeal of WEP and GPO. Whether you agree with it or not, it is now the law of the land. If we can help our oldest Americans achieve a more secure retirement, this repeal should be viewed as a positive development.

CHAPTER 22:

More Social Security Rules to Know

Much of your final decision about Social Security depends on your personal situation at the time you claim. As you've read about other people in earlier chapters, and when they could start Social Security based on their circumstances, I hope you've found some you can relate to.

Before making your final decision about when to claim, carefully review additional rules unique in the Social Security law. These include the following:

1. **The Earnings Limit Test** – This test applies when you're working but decide to claim Social Security before reaching your Full Retirement Age (FRA).

2. **Taxes** – Depending on your overall income, some of your Social Security benefits may be taxed as part of your income at your ordinary income tax rate.

3. **Medicare** – This health insurance program is knitted together as a part of the Social Security law. There are implications to your monthly payment amount when you are enrolled in Medicare and collecting Social Security.

Let's now take a closer look at some key points of each topic so you can better understand how your Social Security payment might be reduced. It's important to read more on Social Security's website and speak with your retirement income financial advisor before making any final decisions.

1. The Earnings Limit Test

Thanks to the inaction of the last several Congresses, people are more worried than ever that Social Security won't be there for them when they need it most. So, they are claiming their Social Security benefits before reaching Full Retirement Age (FRA). They believe this will lock them into some kind of "grandfathered" situation, and if benefits get cut as projected starting in early 2033, their benefit payments won't be affected.

There is no such option. When the reserve account is fully depleted and empty, the only payments that can be made are reduced ones. Social Security, by law, can only pay out up to the amount of payroll taxes it collects plus any reserves. Therefore, everyone's benefits are expected to be cut by about 23% according to the 2025 Social Security Trustees Report projections. There is no grandfathering arrangement.

Those thinking about claiming benefits early understand that Social Security alone won't cover all their expenses. Many plan to continue working for several more years after they claim early benefits. That way, they can keep earning their regular paycheck while also getting extra income by starting Social Security early.

It's actually not a bad idea in theory. The problem is that it doesn't work in real life.

The key point often overlooked is that Social Security is an insurance benefit intended for retirement. If you're still working, well then, you aren't retired!

Here's how the law works

Anyone who qualifies for Social Security retirement benefits can start claiming as early as age 62. In fact, you can even work and earn wages while claiming benefits or have self-employment income. However, if your job pays you too much—above the earnings limit—you won't receive your full Social Security amount. Any benefits exceeding the limit will be withheld until your Full Retirement Age (FRA) and then gradually paid out to you in slightly higher monthly benefits. You will receive the missing payments, but not in a lump sum.

Once you reach your FRA, you can work and claim Social Security. At that time, you'll receive your full benefit without any clawbacks, regardless of how much you earn. This table shows the earnings limit test ranges for 2025:

	In 2025, you may earn up to:	Make more, and benefits are withheld
You are younger than FRA for the entire year	$1,950/mo ($23,400/yr)	$1 for every $2 over the limit
You reach FRA during the year	$5,180/mo ($62,160/yr)	$1 for every $3 over the limit
You reach FRA month	No limit on earnings	Benefits not withheld

An example

Let's say Sally Snowflake was born in December 1962. She turned 62 in December 2024. She'd really like to cut back her work hours because she has a stressful job. She's thinking about moving to part-time and making up some of her lost wages by claiming Social Security. Plus, she is worried that Social Security won't be there for her if she waits until FRA or age 70 to claim.

Today, Sally's gross income is $78,000 working full-time. Her Primary Insurance Amount (PIA) estimate is $2,850; she'd have to wait until her FRA of 67 to receive that benefit amount. If she claims at 62, she would lock in a reduced benefit amount, receiving about $1,995 per month. That's a 30% permanent reduction in monthly income for claiming five years before her FRA.

Sally's income will drop to $48,000 if she goes part-time. She plans to cover most of the $30,000 shortfall by claiming Social Security early. Her reduced benefit is about $24,000 for the year. Or is it?

Remember that Social Security is meant for retired workers, not those who work part-time and claim early to boost their wages. Sally's part-time income of $48,000 exceeds the earnings limit of $23,400. As a result, not all of her Social Security benefits can be paid.

Since she will not reach her FRA this year (she is only 62), any Social Security benefits she claims will be reduced by $1 for every $2 she exceeds the limit. This is the clawback formula.

Sally expected to receive her reduced Social Security benefit of $1,995 per month. Imagine her surprise to find that she'll get $0 from Social Security for January through June. Only in July will her $1,995 payments start. The most she will get in Social Security in the years before reaching her FRA is about $12,000. Not exactly what she had planned.

The earnings limit test has two parts:

1. It reduces the total amount of Social Security benefits the unretired person will receive, and,

2. There are no partial payments made.

That means her $1,995 monthly payment won't be reduced to, say, $1,500 per month. Instead, Social Security only pays allowed benefit amounts each month. And since Sally exceeds the earnings limit, there will be months when she receives $0 until the full clawback has been met.

Keep in mind that Sally is already locking in the smallest Social Security benefit she's eligible for by starting at 62. Then consider the clawback of payments. This probably isn't her best option. Also, if there's a benefit cut beginning in 2033 when the reserve account runs dry, her final payment will be dramatically less than she was thinking.

Last notes about the earnings limit

- Sally doesn't lose her clawed-back benefits. Social Security will recalculate those "lost months" when she reaches her FRA or when she fully retires, whichever happens first.

- In December 2029, Sally will reach her FRA of 67. That year, her benefits might still be withheld, but this depends on her expected earnings. The earnings test is more generous in the year you reach FRA. Social Security acknowledges that many people will be winding down their jobs just before their FRA.

- Once Sally reaches her FRA in December 2029, she can continue working, earn any amount, and receive a recalculated benefit amount. Social Security will restore the months that had been withheld. The overall effect is that her $1,995 monthly reduced benefit will increase.

- Workers never lose the benefits that were clawed back before FRA. However, don't expect a lump-sum check for the months of benefit payments that were missed. Instead, the new post-FRA monthly payments will be higher.

2. Taxation of Social Security benefits

On a flight to Florida, I overheard one woman tell another that, "Once you start Social Security and live in retirement you don't pay taxes anymore." She sounded very authoritative and confident. She couldn't be more wrong.

Unless your income keeps you in the lowest tax bracket, you will indeed pay taxes on any dollars defined as "income" throughout retirement. Your Social Security benefits are considered income in many cases. However, whether you owe taxes on them depends on your overall household financial situation.

Tax on a tax

The general rule for determining the taxation of your Social Security benefits is that if your household "combined income" exceeds a certain threshold, part of your benefits will be taxed.

Many people believe it's unfair to tax a benefit that has already been taxed. You've paid taxes on your income while working and contributed 6.2% of your wages to Social Security, so why are you taxed again on this insurance benefit? In 1983, during the Reagan Administration, an amendment was passed to tax a portion of Social Security benefits for higher-income individuals to help strengthen the program. Unfortunately, the thresholds for defining "high-income" were not indexed for inflation. Each year, more retirees fall into these low-income brackets, which means your benefits are increasingly subject to taxation.

For single tax filers with a "combined income" of $34,000 or more, up to 85% of their Social Security benefits received for the year will be counted as income and taxed as ordinary income.

For married couples filing jointly, if their combined income reaches $44,000 or more, up to 85% of both Social Security payments will be reported on IRS Form 1040 as income.

Whether you need to include up to 50% of your Social Security benefits as taxable income or up to 85% depends on where your combined income falls. Here is the current table of limitations:

Your Tax Filing Status	If Your Combined Income is...	...Then Some of Your Benefits Will be Included in Your Taxable Income
Individual	$25,000–$34,000	Up to 50%
	Greater than $34,000	Up to 85%
Joint	$32,000–$44,000	Up to 50%
	Greater than $44,000	Up to 85%

Figuring out combined income

Combined income is a straightforward calculation. Add together the following amounts on a specific worksheet found in IRS Publication 915: Social Security and Equivalent Railroad Retirement Benefits:

- Your Adjusted Gross Income from line 11 of Form 1040 or 1040SR.

- Any income that is otherwise non-taxable (such as tax-free municipal bonds).

- Half of your yearly gross Social Security income.

- Half of your spouse's gross Social Security income, if you are married and filing jointly.

The sum of these amounts is your combined income. From there, you follow the steps in the worksheet, comparing your combined income to the upper and lower thresholds that determine whether some of your Social Security gets taxed and how much. You'll include the portion of your benefits that must be included as income in box 6b of the 1040.

The bottom line here is: if you've been a good saver and have IRAs and other tax-deferred retirement accounts, or if you plan to work in retirement, or if a significant portion of your investments are in non-taxable interest-bearing investments, it's going to be easy for you to exceed the combined income limits. As a result, a good portion of your Social Security payments will be subject to regular income tax.

You or your tax preparer will need to run this analysis each year. Some years you might owe taxes, and other years you might not. It depends on your combined income each and every year.

Voluntarily withholding taxes from Social Security

If you're likely to owe income tax on your Social Security benefits, you might consider asking Social Security to withhold some taxes from your monthly benefits. There's no requirement to do so, but some people find it easier to pay each month rather than each quarter. Or to write a sizeable check to the IRS in April.

After receiving your first payment, you can file Form W4-V and submit it to Social Security. You simply inform the SSA that you want them to withhold a specific amount for your tax obligation. You can change your withholding at any time by submitting another W4-V.

As with all tax matters, it's a good idea to talk with your tax professional ahead of time.

Didn't Social Security taxation get removed in the 2025 budget bill?

Despite the loud pontification from the president, many members of Congress, and even the new Social Security Commissioner, taxation of Social Security benefits did not change in the final budget bill, HR 1. Your gross Social Security benefits are still included in the combined income calculation. If your income exceeds the thresholds, up to 85% of your Social Security will be reported on line 6b of the 1040 and will increase your taxable income. Full stop.

Now, there were two changes in deductions in the 2025 budget bill that those who are 65 and older may benefit from[15]:

1. The standard deduction has increased beyond the usual cost-of-living adjustment. In 2024, those who were 65 and older and using the standard deduction method (instead of the itemized deduction method) could reduce their taxable income by $16,550 if filing individually or $32,300 for those filing jointly. In 2025, the standard deduction for those 65 and older increased to $17,750 for single filers and $33,500 for joint filers.

2. A new, but temporary, special "Personal Deduction" was added for tax years 2025–2028. This personal deduction is $6,000 for each individual who turns 65 or older in 2025. The new, temporary bonus deduction can be claimed whether the tax filer claims the standard deduction or itemizes. Importantly, they do not need to be collecting Social Security to qualify for this additional deduction. Additionally, other factors will determine if the bonus deduction applies, including:

   • **AGI limits eligibility for the full deduction.** The full $6,000 applies only to single filers with AGI below $75,000 and married couples filing jointly with AGI below $150,000. The deduction will be phased out when AGI is between $75,000 and $150,00 for single filers, and between $150,000 and $250,000 for married filers.

   • **No additional deduction if you are married and filing separately.** If you are married and filing separately, this personal deduction does not apply. However, the new, higher standard deduction amounts do apply.

Bottom line: carefully navigate new deductions

It would be wise to spend more time learning about the new tax provisions starting in 2025. There are some new strategies to lower taxable income for certain seniors. Primarily, these changes benefit lower-income and moderate-income seniors. Any tax breaks for seniors after the last five years of unusually high inflation will be a welcome improvement.

You might find it most helpful to use an online tax software that includes all the new rules and limits. Alternatively, look for an accountant or other tax professional who can assist you in navigating the ever-changing landscape.

At the end of the day, don't confuse temporary, additional tax deductions with the complete elimination of tax on your Social Security benefits. That simply is not true.

3. Medicare and Social Security: Kissin' cousins

Another important factor to consider before claiming your Social Security benefit is how much your Medicare Part B premiums will be. Medicare is not free, much to the surprise of many. There are several parts and pieces to Medicare, each with their own rules and costs. For the purpose of Social Security, Medicare Part B is the part to focus on. Here's why:

The Social Security and Medicare programs are knitted together under the same law. Once you're enrolled in both programs, they work together. The Social Security Administration is responsible for calculating and collecting your Part B premiums. After your individual Part B premium is determined for the year, it will be automatically deducted from your Social Security benefits before payments are deposited into your bank account. You don't have a choice in this. You can't opt in or out. It happens automatically behind the scenes. Think of it this way: you'll never miss a Medicare premium payment, so you don't risk losing this part of your coverage.

The result, however, is a big surprise. You won't receive as much Social Security income as you might have been planning for, and your monthly cash flow will be lower.

What is Medicare Part B?

Medicare Part B is the part of Medicare that helps you pay for your doctors and outpatient procedures once you reach age 65 and no longer have group health insurance from a large employer. There is a long list of items covered under Part B. Ask your doctor and use the tools on www.medicare.gov to find out whether a specific procedure will be covered by Medicare or not.

The best way to think about Part B is that it covers services and supplies that are medically necessary to treat your health condition. It also includes many preventative services and vaccines. You may still have to pay co-pays and deductibles, but generally, Part B covers about 80% of the costs for covered services. That's why you pay a monthly premium— for the 80% covered by Part B. You are responsible for the remaining 20%.

Part B premiums rise much faster than general inflation

The amount you'll pay for your Part B premiums depends on your total household income. Technically, the income used to determine your Part B premium is called "Medicare MAGI." It's your adjusted gross income plus any non-taxable interest income—or Modified Adjusted Gross Income for Medicare.

If your income falls below a base income amount, you'll pay the standard monthly premium for the year. If your income exceeds the base threshold, you will meet IRMAA—Income Related Monthly Adjustment Amounts. These are additional amounts that high-income individuals must pay for their Part B during retirement.

The thresholds change each year, as does the standard Part B premium. Usually, the next year's IRMAA table becomes available around October. Social Security will inform you individually about how much your upcoming Social Security benefit will be, what you will pay for the standard Part B premium, and if you owe any IRMAA upcharges. You'll receive a determination letter late in November or early December, and the new rates start in January.

To give you some examples of how quickly Part B premiums increase, take a look at these couple of recent years:

- The standard monthly premium in 2019 was $135.50, totaling $1,626 for the year. This is a per-person cost, so you'll pay $135.50 each month, and if you're married, your spouse will pay the same amount.

- By 2025, the standard monthly Part B premium had jumped to $185 per person, or $2,220 annually. That's nearly $50 more per month than just five years ago.

Keep in mind that the monthly premium costs typically increase each year. If you haven't started Medicare you can check www.medicare.gov to find the latest premium costs every year. It's important to plan for these increases each year throughout your long retirement.

If your household has a high income, expect to pay significantly more for Part B premiums. Based on your household's modified adjusted gross income, premiums with IRMAA ranged from about $190 per month per person to over $460 per month per person in 2019. In 2025, the premiums including IRMAA ranged from $259 per month per person to over $628 per month per person.

What to do about Medicare?

Medicare is an incredibly important yet wildly complex program. It will be up to you to learn everything you can about how to get your health insurance during retirement and to plan for the rapidly rising costs.

I have two top pieces of advice for you about Medicare and the premiums you'll be paying.

1. Start learning about Medicare by age 60. Spend time digging around on the Medicare website, www.medicare.gov. It is chock-full of information you will need to understand before enrolling.

2. For a much easier way to learn about Medicare, get a copy of my book, Creating Your Medicare Recipe. It breaks down each piece and part of Medicare into the information you need. Most importantly, it covers how you need to approach your own enrollment into Medicare so you can avoid penalties and coverage gaps. You can find my Medicare book on Barnes & Noble and Amazon.

Take the time now to start exploring how you'll get your health insurance in retirement and what it will cost. For many people, it can be an unexpectedly large expense in their retirement budget.

When it comes time to enroll in Medicare, you'll sign up for it on Social Security's website (not on Medicare's website). Make sure you have your MySocialSecurity account set up ahead of time. The process will go much smoother if you have the right pieces in place.

CHAPTER 23:

Final Thoughts

When you think about all your friends, family, and people you know, some are married, some divorced, some widowed, and some single. Some have spouses they like, while others don't. Some have been married and divorced three times by now. Some were widowed young, then remarried, divorced again, and widowed once more. Some might even have a spouse in jail. Spouses can be Green Card holders. Sometimes, young mothers become widowed while their children are still at home.

Bottom line: everyone's life is unique. When it comes to Social Security benefits, it's all about you and your specific situation. Social Security might seem complicated, but this complexity serves important reasons. It's about helping women maintain some independence and dignity in retirement – and retirement can last a very long time for women. It's also about helping men provide income and insurance in retirement for themselves and their spouses. Importantly, Social Security is also designed to help families in crisis after the loss of a wage-earner when there are young children at home.

Social Security is a critically important part of our country's so-cial safety net. For retirees, it offers a form of insurance through monthly benefits earned over time, for the possibility you live a long life.

Will you live till 80?

Of course, no one can know that for sure... unless you're already 80 or older! From a retirement income planning perspective, the general rule of thumb is that you plan for the odds you'll live beyond average life expectancy. For single women who are alive and relatively healthy at 65, their average life expectancy is about age 86, and 25% of them will live well into their 90s. For men who are alive and relatively healthy at age 65, their average life expectancy is about age 83. Fewer will live into their 90s, but that likelihood depends on factors such as health, race, access to medical care, and more.[16]

Married women face even longer odds. A wife has a 50-50 chance of living to 94 and a 25% chance of living to 98 years old.[17] Any way you look at these ages, they indicate a long time in retirement.

If you live a long time in retirement, would you rather have more income from Social Security every month or less? A higher monthly income is better when you reach your 80s, 90s, and even 100.

This isn't to say that everyone should wait until age 70 to claim their benefits. Some people can't wait and need to claim earlier. But remember, claiming too early, at 62, 63, or 64, can have serious long-term consequences, such as:

- Locking in the smallest amount of monthly income now and for your later years in retirement.

- Drawing down and depleting your personal savings faster than you intended, running out of money late in retirement, or reducing your legacy plans.

- If there is a 23% cut to benefits starting around 2033, reduced benefits will provide significantly less monthly income than you need.

- If you are the higher earner in a married couple and you claim early, you lock in a much lower survivor benefit for either yourself or your spouse.

Claiming Social Security is a critical financial decision

Claiming Social Security is one of the most important financial choices you'll make. Few people see it that way, but it's a key part of your financial health as you age and have fewer or no employment options. So, how and when you claim can significantly shape your financial future.

No one in their 80s or 90s is happy to receive less income than they should have. Many simply didn't understand how much they were entitled to receive. They misunderstood their Social Security statement. Or quite frankly, they never thought much about the consequences to their claim.

By age 60, most women are tired. They have experienced many bumps and bruises along their life's path. They want to stop working or change what they are doing. Grandchildren are a strong pull to step away from work and take on the role of granny or nana.

Men are also plenty tired by 60, especially if they have had a physical job during some or all of their working years. The body begins to betray them, and small aches and pains turn into severe arthritis or other painful conditions that force them out of such demanding work.

The reality is you might need to retire in your late 50s or early 60s. And that is okay. Make any necessary life changes to adapt to your situation and prioritize your health. But keep the decision to retire separate and distinct from when you'll claim Social Security. You are making two separate decisions here, and both will have significant consequences for your retirement income.

Now you know

Now that you know you're making two of the most important financial decisions you'll ever make—when to stop working and when to claim Social Security—what will you decide? Both of these major financial decisions are typically made in your early 60s, yet have financial implications for the next 25, 30, 35 years.

That should give you some pause before making either decision and factor into your planning if you're still working for an employer in your 50s. Employers are under no obligation to keep you on the payroll. Many people in their late 50s or early 60s find themselves out of a job. You'll want to plan for that possibility, even if you think it's unlikely.

If you can't find a job at 62 or 63 that pays what you're earning now, what will you do? Claiming Social Security early should not be your first option, as the long-term financial consequences are generally too significant.

Thirteen final take-aways

Let me close this book with a baker's dozen of takeaways that may help you stake your Social Security claim wisely and effectively. Keep in mind that the Social Security law will likely be mixed and kneaded, stretched and strained throughout the rest of the 2020s. But also remember that it is a stable program designed to keep as many Americans out of poverty in their oldest years as possible. It's just lightly toasted and far from being burnt to a crisp!

Here's how to move forward:

1. Sign up for your statement at www.ssa.gov/myaccount and create your mySocialSecurity account. Use your statement to decide how long to work and see how much your monthly income might be.

2. Know all your options for claiming and understand that they may change over time as your marital status changes. From married to divorced to widowed to remarried to widowed...

3. Understand the importance of your Full Retirement Age (FRA). It serves as your anchor for calculating your benefit.

4. Try to wait until your FRA before claiming. You can retire earlier, but wait to claim if possible.

5. Waiting until age 70 is nice, but it only works for a few. You will earn 8% per year in "bonus" money when you claim after your FRA and by age 70.

6. If you claim any benefit before your FRA, you lock in a permanent reduction to your monthly income. Claiming at 62 locks in a permanent reduction of 25%–30% for all your remaining years.

7. While you can work and claim Social Security before FRA, some or all of your reduced benefits will be withheld if you earn more than the Earnings Limit.

8. If you are married and have your own record, make sure you receive your spousal top-up when your spouse begins their claim, if eligible.

9. Make sure you will have sufficient income if you become the surviving spouse.

10. Read, read, read. This material is hard to understand. The language is unusual, and the concepts are not intuitive. It all seems quite complicated at first.

11. Understand that SSA agents are trained to give precise information at specific point in time. They cannot and do not provide strategies for your long-term financial success.

12. Find a financial advisor who specializes in Social Security and developing retirement income plans. It may not be the same advisor who helped you build your nest egg. Interview new advisors and organize your financial house to create sustainable retirement income.

13. When it's time to claim, you can usually do so on www.SSA.gov, but claiming ex-spousal or survivor benefits must be done in person.

I hope you find this information helpful as a starting point. Remember, only the Social Security Administration can tell you your actual benefit amount. Everyone who retires will eventually interact with Social Security. Learning more now should help you make the best decisions for your financial future.

Here's wishing you a happy, healthy, and enjoyable retirement. And that Social Security payments give you a solid financial foundation for your future.

Acknowledgments

This book would not have been possible without the help of so many. My most sincere *thank-yous* go to:

The amazing people I've met around the country who have been surprised by the complexity of Social Security, but who are now taking the time to figure out the best strategies for claiming their own benefits.

My friends and family members who were willing to be interviewed for some of the stories in this book. Each had such interesting situations that represent many people facing similar detours and decisions.

Julie Perry. You are a gem of a friend. You are always on my side, no matter what kind of crazy thing I've come up with. And you throw yourself completely into my book ideas, which keeps me motivated and moving forward.

Judy Tarpley. You were the one who asked me 20-something years ago about claiming at 62 while still working. That was the question that sparked my deep interest in how and why Social Security works the way it does. You never know the power of one seemingly little question.

Geralyn Miller. Can't thank you enough for your amazing design work to support my books and my business. You are the reason I get these books over the finish line. I truly could not finish without your amazing talent. I am even more grateful we've become friends. Thank you for all your support.

Ellen Feinsand and Polly Walker. Originally business colleagues who ended up becoming some of my most trusted friends and confidants. Thank you for all your support, ideas, and shoulders over the past three decades. (But who's counting!)

My wonderful adult children, Katie and Lindsay, who make me laugh. You send the silliest GIFs and texts and pictures of your crazy cats and dog to keep every day light and fun. I am so proud of how you are embracing your financial futures. And yes, I do believe Social Security will be there for your retirements.

Last, but definitely not least, my heartfelt thanks go to my wonderful husband, Dan. I truly appreciate your willingness to be a sounding board for my ideas and that you even made a few dinners (under protest) while I focused on getting just one more chapter done. I have always loved you best. But you are still the one who has to wait until 70 to claim your Social Security benefits!

About the Author

My career passion is all about retirement and how Baby Boomers have been reinventing retirement. I believe every financial decision is a retirement decision – not just the dollars you sock away into your retirement plan at work or an IRA. (By the way, you do have an IRA, right?)

I am a mother, wife, daughter, sister, aunt, and now a great-aunt. The time I spend with my family is what I treasure most.

To date, I've made 16,425 dinners for my family. I'll have another 15,000 or so dinners to make in my retirement years. Hope I'm up to the challenge. I'm an occasional gardener, marching band fan, and ancestor researcher.

In 2005, I founded Mantell Retirement Consulting, Inc., a company focused on retirement business development, marketing, and education that supports financial services firms, advisors, and their clients. I hold two professional designations: Retirement Management Advisor (RMA®) and National Social Security Advisor (NSSA®). I also obtained a Health Insurance License in 2022 and the Elder Planning Specialist in 2025.

My first book, *What's the Deal with... Retirement Planning for Women*, is now in its 2nd edition. For those trying to figure out how to plan for retirement, you'll enjoy my discussion guide and workbook, *Cookin' Up Your Retirement Plan*. It was featured in the Wall St. Journal along with *Creating Your Medicare Recipe*. All my books are available on Amazon and Barnes and Noble.

My blog, Boomer Retirement Briefs at https://boomerretirementbriefs.com, is a fun look at how Baby Boomers are reshaping and redefining retirement. I invite you to send me your retirement ideas on the blog or on Facebook (BoomerRetirementBriefs).

Endnotes

1   SSA Historian's Office; Social Security Fact Sheet for December 2024

2   Center for American Progress, Breadwinning Women Are a Lifeline for Their Families and the Economy, Kennedy Andara, Sara Estep, Isabella Seles-Betsch, May 9, 2025, https://www.americanprogress.org/article/breadwinning-women-are-a-lifeline-for-their-families-and-the-economy/

3   Pew Research Center, In a Growing Share of U.S. Marriages, Husbands and Wives Earn About the Same, by Richard Fry, Carolina Aragão, Kiley Hurst, Kim Parker, April 13, 2023. https://www.pewresearch.org/social-trends/2023/04/13/in-a-growing-share-of-u-s-marriages-husbands-and-wives-earn-about-the-same/

4   Social Security Administration, Fast Facts & Figures About Social Security in 2024

5   Social Security Administration, Historian's Office

6   The 2025 Annual Report of the Board of Trustees of the Federal Old-Age and Survivors Insurance and Federal Disability Insurance Trust Funds

7   SSA Research paper: Improving the Measurement of Retirement Income of the Aged Population, Irena Dushi and Brad Trenkamp, ORES Working Paper No. 116 (released January 2021) https://www.ssa.gov/policy/docs/workingpapers/wp116.html

8   US Census Bureau, 1930 census and https://canvas.santarosa.edu/courses/24761/pages/women-in-the-1930s-and-1940s

9   US Census Bureau 9/17/2023, https://www.census.gov/newsroom/stories/unmarried-single-americans-week.html

10   Ibid.

11   Centers for Disease Control, CDC.gov

12   Pew Research Center, Sept. 2018; BLS, Employment Characteristics of Families – 2018

13   Pew Research Center, The Demographics of Remarriage, by Gretchen Livingston, November 2014, https://www.pewresearch.org/social-trends/2014/11/14/chapter-2-the-demographics-of-remarriage/#fn-40003-9

14   Child Support Statistics in the United States, Annie E. Casey Foundation, June 29, 2024

15   2025 tax and spending bill as passed by Congress and signed into law on 7/4/2025. Known as "One Big Beautiful Bill" or OBBB

16   Centers for Disease Control, Mortality in the United States, 2023, NCHS Data Brief No. 521, December 2024

17   Society of Actuaries longevity estimates

www.ingramcontent.com/pod-product-compliance
Lightning Source LLC
Chambersburg PA
CBHW060453250326
41828CB00037B/962